W9-AFP-676

THE WORLD'S 99 GREATEST INVESTORS
– THE SECRET OF SUCCESS

THE WORLD'S 99 GREATEST INVESTORS
– THE SECRET OF SUCCESS

© Magnus Angenfelt, 2013

Design: Benny Mårtensson

Author photo: Anders Roos

Editor: Brenda Sidemo
and Erika Feldt

Translations: Charlotte Merton

Printed by: ScandBook Falun, 2013

ISBN: 978-91-86691-53-0

Roos & Tegnér

Monbijougatan 17 G

211 53 Malmö

www.roostegner.se

THE WORLD'S

99

GREATEST INVESTORS

THE SECRET OF
SUCCESS

MAGNUS ANGENFELT

ROOS & TEGNER

TABLE OF CONTENTS

THE INVESTORS

'The secret to success in any field is to find what success-ful people do, think about and act on, and do the same.'

ANTHONY ROBBINS

FOREWORD

The quote from Anthony Robbins on the previous page is a good description of my purpose with this book. Charlie Munger, Warren Buffett's legendary business partner, has said for his part that he is more interested in failures than successes. Like many people, I find my memory sometimes fails me, and when a familiar situation arises I don't want to misremember it and draw the wrong conclusions. That is why I stick to reading about the successful examples and analysing them.

If you share this kind of experience you will like this book. In the following pages you will read about the 99 best investors in the world. For each, there is a brief résumé of their investment philosophy and style (and yes, sadly there are only men), and they share their advice and insights garnered from at least 25 years of experience. Taken together, these men represent over 3,000 years of the most successful investment strategies of modern times. Yet the 99 have not limited themselves to advice on how to think and act when investing, for with experience and age comes a willingness to share wisdom about life in general. Even readers who are little interested in investing per se are likely to benefit from reading this book.

There are many books about the investment strategies that have worked best in the past. Computer simulations can pinpoint exactly when you should have bought and sold. There are just two small problems: the markets are constantly changing; and investors are individuals who have mental barriers, no matter how rational they say they are. This book is thus concerned with performance that is practically possible – not just theoretically possible – by flesh-and-blood investors. And I have to admit, it is a performance that goes far beyond impressive. You will not agree with everything; in fact, a great deal of it will go against the grain of your beliefs. Yet that is just as it should be, for there is no one-size-fits-all approach.

The most important thing is to understand the way the most successful investors look at things. If you do that, you will be able to recognize the signs of market change, and can alter your compass bearing accordingly.

Whether a private or a professional investor, the hope is that you will improve your returns by reading the book. In particular, it has a great deal to offer private individuals. History scares people. Several different measurements from around the world show that a majority of individuals lose money on their investments, and do so quite unnecessarily. It seems more difficult to hold onto money than to earn it. Financial ignorance is expensive, and – except for the US – the school system tends to leave citizens in the lurch. That does not bode well for either individual or society.

On average, my chosen 99 investors outperformed the market by about twelve percentage points a year for 25 years. At the time of writing, they each manage an average of $10 billion. If they continue at this rate for another ten years, and the benchmark is zero, they will create an excess return of $1,206 billion to be distributed to clients, themselves, and – as is very evident in this book – charity. By comparison, according to the OECD's Development Assistance Committee, the total global aid budget in 2010 was $127 billion.

The objection to this kind of reasoning, according to many, is that the financial market is not alchemy. Investors cannot make money, they just grab a larger slice of the pie than others – it is a zero-sum game. Yet that idea really doesn't hold water. It is not a zero-sum game for society. Fair enough, it is impossible to measure in exact terms the good investors can do, but with bad investors, for example, we might have had ten parallel railroads in each country and perhaps a hundred car manufacturers producing cars at significantly higher prices than today. Weak businesses and weak industrial structures would be supported overly long, and otherwise viable ventures would be starved of the necessary financing.

The most important factor, however, is that high yields encourage more capital to enter the financial market. Everyone who has money to invest, whether they are individuals, institutions, or companies, wants a good return on their assets. In this search for profits, it is the likes of the investors in this book who serve to funnel the capital flow to entrepreneurs, companies, and countries. The more intelligently money is managed, the better the world's wheels spin.

Successful investors also encourage potential investors to venture into the game, which increases competition and thus, according to all economic theories, improves the outcome for the whole economy. Conversely, the fewer the investors who manage to deliver excess returns, the fewer new investors, which in turn leads to less risk capital and less yield, and so on.

Moreover, you will find evidence here that successful investors contribute to society in many ways. The media usually depict wealthier investors as scrooges, but while that might be an accurate description for some younger investors, both professionally and privately, the successful investors presented here give a completely different picture.

It was the famous German poet and playwright Bertolt Brecht who coined the phrase 'Erst kommt das Fressen, dann die Moral', 'Food first, then morality'. However, most of the investors in this book are nothing like the caricature, in fact many of them give ample proof of an altruistic view of the world

Take only two quotes from the deeply religious Sir John Templeton, one of the most successful global investors in modern times: 'Measure success with a single word – love', and, 'I think God supplies all of our needs if we are trying to help other people, so we do not need to be concerned about our own welfare'. This is a million miles away from the popular metaphor of 'snakes in suits'. Successful investors deserve respect for not throwing away clients' savings on unworkable business models and instead investing the money where the return will be best for both clients and society; the worst investors deserve nothing of the sort.

Although I will question a range of economic theories, my aim here is not to arrive at any absolute truths. The purpose of this book is to learn from the best, which hopefully will result in even better investors. And that can only be good for the world.

Happy reading!
Magnus Angenfelt, Stockholm, December 2012

A PIECE OF CAKE

t actually sounded pretty straightforward. Compile a list of the 99 best investors in the world, and ask them to share their key insights from their long and successful careers in the financial markets. Add a short summary describing each investor's investment philosophy, plus a little light-hearted information about them.

The only thing that surprised me was that no one had come up with this brilliant idea before. I found it hard to imagine a more readable book for both professional and private investors. The answer came soon enough: it was in all respects more difficult and time-consuming than I could ever have imagined.

It was not just a question of googling '99 best investors in the world' and expecting the list to pop up. The few lists that did exist only covered public funds. And later it would turn out that only a minority of the sharpest investors fell into that category; the majority pursued very different forms of investment, often without public transparency, and in many cases only with their own money.

Instead, I had to turn to the contacts I have made over the years to sweep every country for candidates, regardless of the type of investment they worked with. My goal was to find the investors who had the best long-term returns and who had been active in the market for more than 25 years. Moreover, the returns had to be verified.

It was nothing like as easy as I had naively imagined it would be.

US DOMINANCE

As well as finding the 99 best investors in the world, my aim has also been to find the best investors in at least all the largest countries. You might think that the latter came at the expense of the former, and to a certain extent you'd be correct. If absolute returns had been the only factor, some of the investors included here might have been excluded in favour of others. Yet, equally, it is not easy to make a direct comparison between an equity-fund manager in Japan, where stock prices have fallen for almost a quarter of a century, and a hedge-fund manager in the US.

Most of the major countries in the world are represented in the book; however, for some countries - Greece, Venezuela, Malaysia, and others - it proved impossible to find any outstanding investors with a proven track record. Rest assured, I have looked. In total, I have considered several thousand investors.

Lack of experience explains why the book lacks representatives from Eastern Europe and China - it was not until 1980 that China began hesitantly to open the doors to a market economy, while the breakthrough in Eastern Europe came with the fall of the Berlin Wall - although they are at least represented thanks to several very successful emigrants. Two of the most successful investors (George Soros and László Szombatfalvy) are Hungarian by birth, which given the small size of population - fewer than ten million - is remarkable. Hungary wins the country competition, if indirectly. Marc Faber and Mark Mobius represent China. Both are very experienced investors who live in the region, but who grew up and were educated in Switzerland and the US respectively. Michael Hintze, founder and head of the hedge fund CQS, emigrated from China when young.

The geographical mix is clear as it is, and my conclusions would not change if it were different: there is an overwhelming predominance of US-based investors. More than half of the 99 are from the US, and it could have been even more. The country has simply been blessed with a great many talented investors, and there are several reasons for this over-representation. The fact that the US was one of the earliest countries to trade in stocks counts for something, even though the first bourse opened in Bruges in 1309, and debt had been managed in an organized fashion in France back in the thirteenth century. In the twentieth century, while half of Europe slipped into communism and several European countries adopted socialist governments, in the US the door was wide open to the market economy. A cornerstone of the market economy is access to capital and investors. The need to allocate risk capital in the most efficient manner possible demanded an education system that expanded its curriculum to include basic knowledge of investing.

Several of the American investors in this book have said it was school that first woke their interest in investing. School in the 1940s, in other words. Some say that the American investment guru Benjamin Graham was the main reason. He became a teacher and model for a whole generation of American investors. But he too was a product of his time, when the need for venture capital gave birth to a new financial industry. Graham began to teach students about value investing in 1928.

Today, America's schools are visited by famous investors, including Warren Buffett; stimulating speakers that I suspect help attract talented students to join the ranks of the world's best investors. It has until now not been as easy to find either role models or university courses in finance in Europe, Asia, and Africa.

The US has also been more liberal in the regulation of its financial markets, which has made it easier for the industry to expand. The first hedge fund was started in the US in 1949; over half a century later, they are still banned in some European countries.

Neither should we forget the impact of war on financial markets. Investors from, say, Central Europe have a much more conservative investment profile than those from the US. That is why the book has so few investors from Germany and Austria, as they tend to be more risk averse. They often seem to find property and land more interesting than shares.

Other countries should take note of the US experience - particularly that they should not take skilled investors for granted. A successful market economy requires an efficient financial market, which includes the spread of risk capital. Entrepreneurs need capital to start up and to survive. Mature companies need capital to expand. And countries too need capital. The better a country's investors, the better its economy will function, leading to higher living standards and less poverty. The best investors are usually only mentioned when there is discussion of salary rankings or excessive pay. Yet they are more important than that.

WEEDING OUT

The reason I chose to look at long-term success was that I wanted to eliminate the chance that an investor had just been lucky. If someone has generated excess returns for decades, it cannot be put down to mere luck - in fact, luck would have little to do with it. For that reason, I have not included some renowned investors who only made a brief, albeit successful, appearance in the financial markets.

Take, for example, the American hedge-fund star Jeffrey Vinik, who is not one of my 99. His hedge fund posted an astonishing return of over 50 per cent annually for four years. After this success, he closed the fund and returned $4.2 billion to his clients. Now the only money he manages is his own, and he concentrates on other ventures, including sports clubs. Even though he's not included here, I asked him to share his three most important insights from his own particular angle. These are his conclusions:

★ Play your cards as they come out of the deck; make your investment decisions based on all available information; do not anticipate.
★ Respect risk; limit your losses; live to fight another day.
★ Long over short; that's where the big money is made.

Another well-known hedge-fund star notable by his absence is John Paulson. He became a legend and a dollar multi-billionaire for having positioned himself carefully in the run-up to the debt crisis in 2008, and then the following year having gone in to buy what had survived. But before and after that manoeuvre, returns had been mediocre. In 2011, his Advantage Plus Fund lost over 50 per cent and his largest fund - Advantage Fund - does not reach double-digit annual returns averaged over the past 15 years.

Some may raise an eyebrow that Bill Gross, the king of bonds, has not been included. The answer is that neither he nor any other investor who solely focuses on bonds has made the cut. Their returns are simply too poor. My intention has been to compile a list of those who have produced the highest absolute returns, regardless of investment style. Not even the best bond investor can reach double-digit returns in the long term, and this despite the fact that bonds have actually outperformed shares over the past thirty years. Stock guru Peter Lynch once said that he felt sorry for bond investors because they didn't know what they were missing. I can only agree.

This weeding out means that many traders who achieved great returns for a short time have not been included. Few have managed to keep up those levels of returns for long. It seems to be exhausting to track stock rates year in, year out. Value investors in the style of Walter Schloss, Anthony Bolton, and Benjamin Graham have done so tirelessly for decades, and are therefore over-represented here.

With hindsight, several investors proved to be phonies. Among them were the epic swindler Bernard Madoff and the hedge-fund manager convicted for insider dealing, Raj Rajaratnam of the Galleon Group. Setting the bar at a minimum of 25 years experience and relying only on documented income has hopefully reduced the risk of including out-and-out criminals in the book.

The first printed edition included Steve A. Cohen who is the founder of the American hedge fund SAC Capital. He has delivered annual returns of nearly 30 per cent for 20 years. Although the greatest returns were made when the fund was modest in size (it is now $15 billion), his performance is impressive. But after Securities and Exchange Commission (SEC) recently charge companies linked to Cohen $604 million I removed him from the book. If you are involved in the largest insider trading case ever – and also made a settlement with SEC – you should not be a model for the next generation of investors.

CRASHES

Several big names are missing because they went belly-up and were unable to stage a comeback. Victor Niederhoffer was named the world's best hedge-fund manager in 1996, after having produced annual returns of 35 per cent for six years. The following year, he was forced to close his fund. In his second attempt, between 2001 and 2007, the returns were over 50 per cent a year before huge losses again forced him to close the fund. He, like many others, had failed to manage the risks, and therefore does not qualify for inclusion.

Another example is the Swiss shares activist Martin Ebner. He eliminated himself from the list by his disastrous investment in the engineering company ABB. ABB was nearly brought down along with Martin Ebner's own investment empire.

EXCEPTIONS

In looking at success, I have not differentiated between investments in commodities, bonds, currencies, stocks, or businesses. What I have tried to avoid are business builders - a very different discipline. Some may question why then Carlos Slim is included in the book, but Slim, the Mexican entrepreneur and world's richest man, actually started as an investor in the stock market and remains a dominant player there.

Another exception is the American investor John Bogle, who has never delivered returns that outperformed the S&P 500. He is very much the odd one out in this line-up, and by rights should not be included, for he was the originator of index funds, and remains a strong advocate of cheap, passive index funds rather than active fund management, counter to almost every other opinion in this book; however, he has condensed his sixty-year-long investing career and unmatched experience into thoughts and conclusions I simply could not bring myself to withhold from readers. He is a champion of the small investor. Do not miss his insights (p. 56).

My inclusion of the legendary trader Jesse Livermore, who went bankrupt several times, may seem inconsistent. But by scraping together a fortune of $2.5 billion (in today's money) from pure speculation, his investment strategy remains required reading for today's traders. Yet by the same token, I cannot include the American portfolio manager Bill Miller. He beat the comparable index for 15 consecutive years with managed assets that at times exceeded $20 billion. If he had stopped when he was at the top, he would have been hailed as a hero. Instead he continued, read the market wrong during the financial crisis of 2008, and for the last six years of his 28 years in the driver's seat lost against the benchmark. His insights and advice are perhaps even more interesting now as a result. Here they are:

★ Lowest average cost wins.
★ If it's in the newspapers, it's in the price.
★ 100 % of the information you have about a company represents the past, 100 % of its valuation depends on the future.
★ Financial crises are not caused by people borrowing to buy risky assets; they are caused by people borrowing to buy assets they thought were safe, but that turned out to be risky.

The requirement for staying power explains why almost none of the investors are younger than 50. Brilliant young investors such as the Americans Chase Coleman and Lee Ainslie do not yet have the experience to warrant inclusion here. However, no rule without an exception. The Brazilian fund manager Fabio Alperowitch (born 1971) was simply too good to leave out. He has delivered an average return of 34 per cent annually for 19 years - phenomenally successful, in other words.

In a few cases it has been impossible to verify the figures for the returns. This is the case with two American investors, William J. O'Neil and Ed Seykota, yet both have so many successful followers who have used their models that I have contented myself with second-hand information. The same is true of the American investing legend Philip Fisher, but in his case there are sufficient indirect sources. Warren Buffett feels believable.

However, I have not been able to verify the returns produced by four other past investors - the Americans Gerald Loeb and Bernard Baruch, the German André Kostolany, and the Hungarian-born Nicolas Darvas. All of them were also successful writers, and when I tried to obtain data it transpired that at least a couple of them were better writers than investors.

Likewise, I have not managed to include Michael Marcus, the now retired American trend-following commodities trader who reportedly - but unverifiably - transformed $30,000 into $80 million in just 20 years at the end of the last century.

Another investor I have had to leave out is the South African Alan Grey. He is probably Africa's best investor with a return of 27 per cent annually over the past 14 years. Include the period back to 1974, when he began, and the numbers are even better - but unverified. He is now retired and lives in Bermuda.

Eleven investors are no longer with us, four of them having died during the writing of this book. I'm glad I had the opportunity to communicate with the American investor Walter Schloss a few months before he died in the spring of 2012. For others, such as Benjamin Graham, I have relied on public sources.

Probably the best investor in the Arab world and one of the world's wealthiest individuals, Nasser Mohammed Al-Kharafi, sent me his insights, but unfortunately died before I could talk to him about his investment strategy. His three pieces of advice are given on page 252.

UNDER THE RADAR

Six investors for various reasons chose not to participate in the book and it was impossible to find relevant secondary information; however, they would all have qualified for inclusion by a broad margin. All are media-shy American hedge-fund managers.

Ian Cumming and Joseph S. Steinberg are the successful duo behind the American investment company Leucadia. By buying troubled companies at discount prices and then restructuring and reselling them, they have increased the book value per share by an average of 20 % per year over 43 years, compared with 10 % for the S&P 500. Leucadia has been nicknamed a 'mini Berkshire Hathaway' and has a straightforward strategy:

★ Don't pay too much.
★ Buy companies that offer products or services that people need or want.
★ Secure gains are more valuable than taxable profits.
★ And again, don't pay too much.

It sounds so easy, but few have succeeded.

David Shaw founded in 1988 the global quantitative hedge fund D. E. Shaw, which currently manages some $20 billion and generates its profits from small pricing anomalies in the market.

On average, it only retains its positions for a couple of weeks. Despite his success – 14 % annually since inception – Shaw, nicknamed 'King Quant', tired of the whole business of fund management, and has said he felt more of an imbecile for every year that passed. He has now returned full time to research in computational biochemistry. It would have been interesting to hear his thoughts on investing.

Stephen Mandel, who started Lone Pine Capital in 1997, was a disciple of the famous hedge-fund guru Julian Robertson (p. 172). He was a consumer analyst, but also sat on the board of the Tiger Management Corporation. Thorough analysis is his hallmark, technology his favourite sector. Since he began, he has delivered an average 23 % annual return against 6 % for the S&P 500.

Bruce Kovner is a former taxi driver and trader who now runs the hedge fund Caxton Global Investments with $10 billion under management. Kovner excels at steering a large macro fund when uncertainty is at its greatest. He seems to have succeeded pretty well, to put it mildly. For 28 years he has delivered an average 21 % annual return, twice as much as the comparable index.

Louis Bacon founded the hedge fund Moore Capital in 1990. With $13 billion to its name, his is now the second largest macro hedge fund in the world. Despite its size, Bacon has managed to deliver a 31 % average annual return since that start, three times better than the comparable index, and all relatively low-risk, stable returns. Nothing if not amazing.

SOURCES, FIGURES, BENCHMARKS

This book is based on the investors' own information, public records, and my own analyses and conclusions. The insights and advice are taken from the investors themselves. In a few cases, where the investors were unavailable for comment for whatever reason, I have had to rely on public statements, always taken from contexts where they were discussing that particular issue.

The investors are presented in alphabetical order. Each entry begins with the investor's insights and advice. The originals varied considerably in length, from just three sentences to several pages, which I have had to shorten.

When it comes to returns, I have used the latest available figures. For some that means 2010, for others 2011 or 2012, but due to the long period measured the terminal date has not changed the picture significantly.

For some investors there are no official figures available, at which point I have been forced to rely on credible sources in the form of newspaper articles and the like. My ambition has been to give returns gross of fees for better comparability, but in several cases, those figures have been impossible to obtain.

Some investors have managed nothing but their own money, which means no figures for returns are available. In those cases, I have used official wealth statistics for comparison with the investor's own data.

As benchmarks, I have used the most relevant indices. The US investors have been measured against the S&P 500, a stock market index; for local fund managers, I have used local indices; for global investors, the MSCI World Index. In some cases, I have used the benchmark used by the investors, as when they have operated in multiple classes of assets and use a weighted benchmark. Although I have checked thousands of names, there may well be investors that I have missed, and, most likely, some readers will question why certain names have been included and others not. All in all, however, there is no better list than this. Anywhere.

CONCLUSION

It was George Soros who said, 'The fascinating thing about investments is that there are so many different ways to succeed.' That is
the moral of this book in a nutshell. The path to becoming a successful investor is not lined with miraculous universal formulas.
This book contains about as many strategies as there are investors.
Let's look at some examples:

★ Some investors never meet company management (Walter
  Schloss). Others believe it's essential to have close ties with
  management (Shuhei Abe).
★ Some investors choose only to invest in shares that have
  recently reached an all-time high and are set to continue
  to rise (William O'Neil), while others avoid investing unless
  the shares have reached bottom and are generally unpopu-
  lar (J. Kristoffer Stensrud).
★ Some won't invest outside their home country (Ralph
  Wanger), others prefer to look worldwide (Mark Mobius).
★ There are investors who focus on a few investments (Louis
  Simpson) and others who have over a thousand positions
  (Peter Lynch).
★ A few investors prefer to buy and hold onto stock for decades
  (Shelby Davis), while there are some whose time horizon is
  a month at most (Michael Steinhardt).
★ Some investors always follow trends (Marty Zweig), others
  are contrarians (Carl Icahn).
★ Some investors recommend leaving the market when the
  odds are low and the range of decent investment opportuni-
  ties is poor (Jim Rogers), others do not agree, claiming that
  there are always opportunities (Robert Wilson).
★ Some investors prefer to invest in assets linked to consumer
  products (Thomas Russo), others reject them completely
  (Philip Fisher).

★ Some investors assume that history and the markets repeat themselves (Jeremy Grantham), while others take positions in the belief that there are always new directions (James Simons).

★ For some investors, global macroeconomics is the thing (George Soros), while others leave it open (Chetan Parikh).

★ Many investors base their analysis entirely on historical figures (Benjamin Graham), and others concentrate solely on future projections (John Neff) or a combination of both (Anton Tagliaferro).

What is remarkable is that all the investors in this book have earned a great deal of money, despite their wildly different strategies. They all have one thing in common, however: they stick firmly to their principles – in the short term. None of these investors change tack from one day to the next. If something goes wrong, they would rather shut up shop for a while than tinker with their investment philosophy.

When the American investment guru Walter Schloss realized that Benjamin Graham's model, which he himself based his investments on, had become too popular with the market, he closed his fund of 50 years' standing and returned the capital to its customers. Two other American legends – Warren Buffett and Michael Price – have done the same thing, albeit they then started up again at a later stage.

Note, though, that this discipline and firmness of principle applies only in the short term. In the longer term, it is more the rule than the exception that investors adapt to changes in the market. This is perhaps the single most important lesson to be learned from studying the best investors. Only a very few have found a narrow niche where they have been able to operate undisturbed by the competition, able to keep to their strategy come hell or high water. Clinging grimly to a favoured strategy is quite simply not a

proven route to success. Instead, it is flexibility and responsive-
ness to change that is the winning formula. This is what Ken Fisher
means by his pithy remark, 'everything changes'.

The investors in this book seem generally to be pragmatism
incarnate, with no time for obsolete strategies, no time for senti-
mentality. There is by no means an illogical approach. As one of
the greatest economists of all time, John Maynard Keynes, put it,
'When the facts change, I change my mind.'

Even the leading light of investment theory – Benjamin Graham
– changed strategy when he realized that time had caught up on his
original model. Another, more recent example is Warren Buffett.
He seems quite resolute in his investment model, but still shows
flexibility when market conditions change. In the beginning,
Buffett was a value investor pure and simple. These days he is partial to quality companies. What's more, for much of his career he
has excluded technology companies from his portfolio, because of
the difficulty of predicting the future of technological innovations
and the like. Then, suddenly, at the ripe old age of 81 he changed
his mind. In 2011, he bought a 5.5 % stake in IBM and became the
company's largest shareholder.

Another example is the Spanish investor Francisco García
Paramés (who often gets referred to as 'Europe's Warren Buffett').
Despite having delivered double the return compared to a benchmark index for nearly two decades, he decided to change his
approach. Henceforth investments were only to be made in high-
quality companies and so-called value investing went by the board,
even though there were substantial discounts on assets. The grand
old man of Anglo-American investing, Sir John Templeton, began
short selling for the first time in conjunction with the dot-com bubble at the turn of the century. He was then 88 years old and was said
to have made $85 million in the process. An impressive display of
new thinking combined with a good deal of self-assurance. It is easy
to draw a parallel to the standard paraphrase from the theory of

evolution: 'It is not the strongest of the species that survives, nor the most intelligent, but rather the one most adaptable to change.'

Another surprise is the investors' risk-taking and views on risk. It might be tempting to think that the best results come from taking the greatest risks. You'd be wrong. The complete opposite is true. Low risk-taking and careful risk management are common to almost all the investors here.

However, it is not just the ability to be risk averse and flexible in their investment strategy when the market changes that unites them. The fact is that there is such a thing as a successful investor profile. Regardless of the strategy used. Regardless of the market. Regardless of the period. Below are the twelve insights common to virtually all investors.

★ Know your own investment rhythm.
★ Know your strengths and weaknesses.
★ Consider the risks, not the potential.
★ Be prepared to change your strategy if the market changes.
★ Don't invest on the basis of tips.
★ Don't let your emotions cloud your judgement.
★ Don't invest in what you don't understand.
★ Be disciplined and work hard.
★ Only do business with reputable companies and guard your reputation.
★ Don't underestimate the efficiency of the market, but don't overestimate its perfection.
★ It's not wrong to make mistakes, but it is wrong to fail to learn from them.
★ Patience is a virtue, in investing as in all else.

It is far more important to embrace this general advice than to attempt to copy a successful investor's strategy to the letter. The world of investing is not that simple. If a given strategy is successful, it will eventually become overcrowded and stop working. This was always the case in the past. The difference now is that methods become obsolete faster.

The key is to try to understand the successful investor's outlook. And let things take time – investing is not a sprint. It is symptomatic that the American investor John Rogers's company logo is a turtle. And given most investors' age, there's no rush. You're not going to reach the peak of your powers at the age of 25.

Over a quarter of the fund managers were or remain active well beyond the age of 70, and fully 10 % after they had turned 80. It almost seems as if their work promotes longevity. The American investor Irving Kahn (whose performance place him outside the scope of this book) is over 107 years old and still goes to work in Wall Street every day. The same is true of another centenarian, Philip Carret, the investor in this book who holds the record for the longest period managing a specific fund: 55 years.

When Louis Simpson, a hugely successful American investor who worked closely with Warren Buffett, resigned at the age of 74, he immediately started a new investment company. Both Glenn Greenberg and Martin Whitman began new investment ventures when well into their sixties. Investing seems to be the ideal activity if you want to live long and stay alert. Investors tend to show a real enthusiasm for their work. Most seem to love their job, and their curiosity knows no age limits as well as no bounds.

Yet this is not true of them all, for there is a dividing line between short-term and long-term investors. Unsurprisingly, it seems the higher the investment turnover rate, the more exhausting and stressful the work. The exception is George Soros, who has aged with dignity in a challenging branch. The other 'old-timers' in the book invest almost exclusively in the long term in stable, secure assets.

It is not just that the majority of the investors seem tireless. They also began cultivating their interests, and indeed their careers, early. The record holder is probably the American hedge-fund manager Daniel Loeb, who says he became interested in stocks and shares as a five-year-old – almost too strange to be true. Ray Dalio, who heads the world's largest hedge fund, and Carlos Slim, currently the world's richest person, bought their first shares at the age of twelve. Another precocious investor is the Australian Kerr Neilson, who off his own bat became a shareholder at the age of 13. When Warren Buffett was 11 he bought his first shares and played stock markets with one of his sisters.

For those among you who had a more ordinary attitude towards shares as children, it's still not too late. There is also evidence to the contrary, if not quite as much. One example is James Simons, the American who started and ran one of the most profitable hedge funds in the world. He was 40 before he began his investment career. Yet, judging by the investors represented in this book, it does seem to be an advantage to start at a tender age.

100 PER CENT MEN

If you want to be a successful investor, it seems you'll be at something of an advantage if you arrange to be born male and of Jewish descent. Despite my best efforts, it has been impossible to find any women fund managers who meet the criteria for inclusion in this book. Two American investors, Thyra Zerhusen and Susan Byrne, have produced better returns than many men, but not good enough to qualify for a place here. Not even the most famous female investor in history, Hetty Green (1836–1916), made the cut. 'The Witch of Wall Street' was the wealthiest woman of her day, a position she did not only achieve by astute investments. The stories of her parsimony are legion. She never used hot water, for example. Hetty Green managed to yield an average return of 6.5 % per annum for 52 years.

The absence of women from among the 99 considered here is

no surprise, however. In the investment industry's Formula 1 – hedge funds – only 3 % of fund managers are women. One might be tempted to jump to the conclusion that the qualities of a successful investor are not those that appeal to women. Ultimately, an investor has to take risks, and risk-taking, according to some researchers, is not one of women's main characteristics.

Fair enough, that might be true of certain investment strategies, but the profile of the investors in this book point in a different direction. Risk-limiting behaviour and absence of reckless investments are the very things that have made them successful. In other words, this ought to be a profession that suits women. And sure enough, there is evidence that women with a lower tolerance for risk are more successful investors. Back in 2001, a study by Brad Barber and Terrance Odean found that women on average produced an annual return that was 1.4 percentage points higher than men's. Other research findings point in much the same direction, showing that women are even further ahead. Low trade intensity, less impulsivity, and more thorough analysis characterizes women's investments. Exactly the things that pay off in the long run.

In all probability it's tradition and nothing else that explains women's absence from the group covered in the book. I am convinced that things will be different in 25 years' time.

Seen from another perspective it is possible to make another observation – that almost one third of the investors in this book are of Jewish descent.

Without claiming to have any scientific proof it is tempting to make historical connections. For many centuries Jews were forbidden to own real property in Europe.This excluded them from being freeholders and from acquiring land and property, both of which were the greatest investment objects of the time. Jews were simply forced to find other ways of making a living, preferably ones that they could practise even when they needed to move around, since pogroms were common. Thus trading proved to be a suitable occupation for them. It is possibly in the light of these skills passed on from generation to generation that today's overrepresentation of Jewish investors is to be seen.

IQ OF 125 OR LESS

Another advantage, or perhaps condition, is a high level of education. More than one in ten investors in the book have doctorates. One in three has a Master's, almost always with top marks. And not from degree mills either: over half have graduated from the world's most prestigious universities.

As always, however, there is some comfort for the academically uninterested to be drawn from the statistics. A handful of investors had no further education at all (Walter Schloss, Arnold van den Berg, Michael Farber, Jesse Livermore, and Albert Frère). Carl Icahn, Paul Tudor Jones, John Henry, and Sir John Brierley all dropped out of university.

From the selection in the book, no connection between a doctorate and investment returns can be inferred. Warren Buffett once said that success doesn't correlate with IQ beyond a level of 125 – everything above that is of little use.

If it were possible to create the best fund management team with the help of an IQ test, and so put together the best organization, it would already have happened. The hedge fund Long Term Capital was probably the first and last attempt. The fund was established in 1992 by two Nobel laureates in economics, Robert Merton and Myron Scholes. Six years later it was liquidated under traumatic circumstances having lost $4.5 billion. Intelligence seems not to be the most important talent in this line of business.

But regardless of their education and intelligence, as investors they all have one thing in common: they've practiced, long and hard. Almost always close to or under the supervision of an older mentor. On average, most of them have had 15 years of dry runs before setting up shop themselves. Think of Michael Price, an icon on Wall Street, who has said that it took years of practice and thinking before he hit upon his winning investment formula.

Not only that, for the road to a successful model is usually punctuated by a series of failures. Foul-ups and debacles are virtually the rule in the early years. The American investor Charles M. Royce, for example, lost 40 % in his first year managing the Pennsylvania Fund.

Perhaps the author Malcolm Gladwell's assertion in his bestseller Outliers is also true of the investing profession – it takes 10,000 hours of strenuous training to become a star. Probably the learning curve is steeper if you have the chance to study at the feet of an established investment guru. Similarly, it is also probably quicker to assimilate knowledge as a trader than as a fundamental investor. But forget the idea that you could walk in off the street and be a star investor from day one. It's never happened, and it's not going to happen. Ever.

All told, there's good and bad news. Good because there is an opportunity for anyone who is reasonably talented to get ahead, no matter what their style or profile. Bad because there are no shortcuts – it takes hard work, perseverance, and dedication.

Ultimately, you have to be faithful to your mental rhythm. If you get your kicks from there being a lot of investment action, then you should head for the trading corner, not for the long-term investor's pile of well-thumbed annual financial reports – that really wouldn't work out. The investors in this book cover the entire spectrum. It's just a matter of choosing the style that suits best.

IS THE MARKET REALLY EFFICIENT?

One bone of contention in financial markets for the last hundred years is whether the market is efficient or not. The findings presented here do little to strengthen the thesis of the efficient market.

On the contrary. If the market were efficient, no one would be able to beat it in the long run. If anyone were to succeed in doing so, it would only be regarded as luck.

One consequence of this reasoning would be, for example, that this book would be pointless: there would be no need of models, strategies, or advice from successful investors. According to the efficient market hypothesis (EMH), shares are always traded at the correct value. By definition no shares sold are undervalued, no shares bought are overvalued. This means that you cannot deliver a better return than the market, or even time the market right by choosing shares well. This has been the most popular academic position in the last fifty years. Yet it is at odds with the view of most professional investors. Philip Carret, Walter Schloss, William J. Ruane, and all the other long-lived high-yield investors in the book have proved the contrary. And it's not just a few small-scale fund managers we're talking about here; it's nearly a 100 investors who year after year, for an average 25 years, have beaten the market by miles. And usually with less risk.

True, their number may be small, but the capital they're managing is anything but. Even if we exclude investors who are not active in the public market, the total assets under management are more than a trillion dollars. My ambition here is not to refute the EMH thesis; however, the sums involved are too great to be dismissed as a statistical residual.

Instead, my findings should encourage investors to work even harder to beat the market, and customers to seek out the managers who are outliers. It is entirely possible. The market is really not that efficient, after all. Perhaps because ultimately it consists of individuals who are affected by and have an effect on others. Think only of the stock market's dot-com bubble in the year 2000. There was no fundamental, rational explanation for the high values. It was all just emotion.

AND THE SECRET OF SUCCESS IS –

Now to the core issue. What works best, and which investors are considered to be the best? To begin with, it's interesting to see which types of assets are held by the investors in this book – a ranking perhaps best understood from the table below.

Shares	84 %
Bonds	22 %
Commodities	19 %
Derivatives/futures	18 %
High-risk debt securities	6 %

Not surprisingly, shares predominate. The explanation is partly historical. For the past century, shares have yielded an average annual return of about 10 %, while bonds have only managed half that. But it is not the whole truth. For the last 30 years (1981–2011), bonds have enjoyed better returns than equities, and this despite the stock market rally at the end of the twentieth century.

Instead, it mostly comes down to the fact that it is easier to make a difference in the stock market than in the bond or currency markets. Since this book only considers absolute returns (as the saying goes, you can't eat relative performance), it is understandable that more than 80 % of the investors concentrate partially or solely on the stock market.

In terms of the size of the types of assets, however, the stock market is not the obvious choice. Despite there being some 46,000 quoted shares traded worldwide to the tune of a market value of some $50 trillion, the stock market is only half as large as the bond market. The bond market also has three times the number of listed securities. The largest is the foreign exchange market, with a turnover nearly thirty times greater than the stock market.

VALUE INVESTORS RULE!

When it comes to investment strategies, there is no doubt that, among those included in this book, value investors are in a clear majority. In setting out all the investor profiles as a table, it should be noted that boundaries are not hard and fast: an investor can have several different styles, while the various strategies to some extent overlap.

Value	52 %
Contrarian	25 %
Quality	22 %
Growth	20 %
Quantitative	13 %
Trader	12 %

In an article from 1984 in the Columbia Business School Magazine, Warren Buffett took up cudgels for value investing, arguing that it is the best investment strategy. He wrote that 'If a substantial share of these long-term winners belong to a group of value investing adherents, and they operate independently of each other, then their success is more than a lottery win; it is a triumph of the right strategy.' This favours investors who have been active in the market for many years, to the advantage of investors who have a long-term investment horizon and survive the vagaries of short-term trading. The levels of risk are also lower, unless they have highly leveraged assets, which is rare.

Value investing calls for the manager to invest in a company at a price that is lower than the intrinsic value – the origin of the American expression 'Pay 50 cents for a dollar'. Over time, this strategy has proved to offer the most enduring, highest long-term returns. Yet, even so, there have been long periods when it has not done well; between 1990 and 2000, for example, when growth stocks, especially in technology companies, were the rage.

After the dot-com bubble burst in 2000, the value-based approach to investing came back into vogue again. And the question is whether it has ever been as popular as it is now. Every year the best part of 40,000 shareholders make the pilgrimage to the annual shareholders' meetings of Warren Buffett's Berkshire Hathaway in the small city of Omaha to listen to the foremost – and most successful – representative of value investing.

That said, it should be noted that most of the value investors in this book have developed their own versions of value investing, different from the basic model coined by Benjamin Graham. That, and the fact that the long stretches when value investing fared poorly were the reason why the strategy survived in the first place. If it were always the best approach, it would never have lasted; competition would have eroded returns. Choosing the right strategy is not sufficient to get the winning ticket. History is full of less successful value investors.

In the stock market, two popular strategies – value and growth – tend to overlap. One surprise finding here is that not more growth investors qualified for my list: only one in five of the 99 spend all or part of their time investing in growth companies. That proportion would probably be greater had I been writing this in the spring of 2000, just before the dot-com bubble burst. In a historical perspective, however, value investing has beaten growth investing by about 30 % over the past century.

The second commonest is contrarian investing, the strategy used by one in four investors in the book. Put simply, the strategy is based on investing in the things no one else wants. That's the moment to buy, for their valuations are depressed, while the chance of sentiment changing in your favour is greater than if you were to invest in sought-after stocks where valuations are high.

The majority of the world's investors are almost pathologically obsessed with what other investors are up to. The result is an elaborate game of follow-my-leader through the financial markets. This leads to market prices being driven above or below their justified value – and that is what contrarian investors exploit. However, it is easier in theory than in practice, and for a very good reason.

The nightmare scenario for most investors is to be alone in making a mistake. It's not easy to swim against the current. Strength of character, conviction, and perseverance are just a few of the qualities required for success. Sometimes it can take years before the reward comes in the form of a revaluation. It is undoubtedly a risky strategy, and not for the timid. Probably its most famous name is the American investor David Dreman, author of the book *Contrarian investment strategies*. He went against the consensus and invested in bank shares in early 2008 – a large reason why he is not in this book.

Two other strategies – quantitative and quality – are in principle opposed to each other. The quantitative investor, for example, purchases the 'cheapest' shares measured in terms of price–earnings ratio, dividend yield, or asset pricing, regardless of the management of the company, market share, or other 'soft' factors.

The qualitative investor doesn't mind so much about the figures; he's looking for the best company in terms of management, products, and position. Another difference is that you need multiple positions in the quantitative approach, and even more mathematical skill than in microeconomics.

Qualitative investors are more numerous than quantitative investors, but it should be added that several strategies use quantitative models in the initial stages of their analyses. Charlie Munger, Warren Buffett's long-standing partner, has said that it is investments in quality companies that are behind Buffett's success.

Given how obvious it is what works in the long term, it is surprising that there aren't more among the 99 who favour the quantitative approach. Look at stock market returns since 1930, and it is obvious that shares with a low price–earnings ratio offer a better rate of return than those with high price–earnings ratios.

The same goes for high yield versus low yield, as well as pricing the assets of a company. The results are plain. The problem is that there are periods when it hasn't worked. These days, now customers are less likely than before to accept longish periods of underperformance, fewer and fewer investors seem able to invest for the long term.

I had also expected to see several small-cap investors in the list. Over the past 85 years, small and medium-sized companies have delivered significantly better returns than large listed companies. The difference is roughly three percentage points per annum. It may not sound like much, but after nine decades with an annual return of thirteen instead of ten, there is ultimately a tenfold difference. Yet among the 99 just as many focus on big companies as on small and medium-sized ones.

Another approach that is conspicuous by its absence is so-called activist investing. Fewer than 10 % of the investors try to influence the progress of their investments by exerting pressure on company management and boards. It is undoubtedly a time-consuming activity, but extremely profitable for those who are skilled at it. Carl Icahn and T. Boone Pickens are two of them.

SHORT-LIVED TRADERS

If your plan is to get rich quick and you're not interested in growing old in harness – and if you have the talent and the mental rhythm required – then you've little choice: you should become a trader. No other strategy can produce such high returns in such a short time.

The American trader Ed Seykota showed a return of 95 % annually for twelve years. The figure is not verified, but has been quoted so many times that we can assume that it's true. Even if the results were only half as good, it would still be a fantastic achievement. One of Seykota's disciples, Michael Marcus, is reported to have delivered a 48 % average annual return for 20 years!

One can but wonder what sort of dispositions these individuals must have to enable them to produce such results. Although there are a few traders who have doctorates, it would seem that academic education is not as important to them as it is to other types of investor. Indeed, of the investors among the 99 who did not go on to higher education, the majority are indeed traders. Psychological insight and courage are important tools of the trade, not so a knowledge of macro- or microeconomics.

But you get what you pay for. This strategy is both risky and exhausting. Few investors manage to keep it up for long. The most experienced of all, the renowned American speculator Jesse Livermore, struggled with depression later in life and ultimately committed suicide.

The traders' strategies demand an approach and skills that are the very opposite of those of value investors, yet, as this book shows, they can be just as successful. What is crucial, however, that they are applied by an investor with the right mindset. Possibly it's also a little easier to absorb the necessary knowledge for a successful trading strategy than it is to fully understand the theories of value investing, but, again, you still have to have the right mentality.

Traders have a soft spot for trends, they take their losses in time, and they let their profits run, but few of them are notably successful at speculating on market direction, regardless of which type of asset they are interested in – a somewhat surprising finding. For example, virtually all the studies show that fully 60 % of the return on a share depends on how the stock market as a whole fares. By rights, it ought to be more profitable and more important to be correct about the market's direction than to spend time identifying the right shares to buy. In reality, the opposite is true. If we assume that the market is rational, the simple explanation is then that it is incredibly difficult to judge how the market will develop.

Instead, the specific movements in currency, equity, or derivative markets often explain investors' excess returns. It seems that the legendary economist John Maynard Keynes's tart remark that 'Markets can remain irrational a lot longer than you and I can remain solvent' is often borne out in reality.

Generally speaking, the investors in this book do not display a prodigious talent for timing. Many are the examples when they have stepped away too early or too late. The American investor Jeremy Grantham of GMO began to get cold feet about technology companies as early as 1995, and instead upped the cash holdings in the portfolio. The price for being too early was to see the fund halved in size as frustrated shareholders took their money elsewhere.

Grantham's analysis and behaviour was shared by several people in the book. Yet they, on the other hand, lost nothing when the dot-com bubble burst a few years later. And, in contrast to many other more daring investors, they are still active. In fact, only a few investors among the 99 lost money at the turn of the century. That alone is enough to make them unique.

However, it is not only hard facts and strategies that distinguish between or unite investors. Attitude is just as important. One feature that I have found to be common to all the investors considered here is a general awareness of the problems that can arise.

Several of them see problems at every turn and are constantly worried. Some, like Philip Fisher, are always worried about their investments. For some, the uncertainty and turmoil is a source of even greater satisfaction when things go right. It gives them a humble attitude to work. Ultimately, it is an anxiety born of critical thinking. A healthy fear.

Another form of behaviour that stands out is their set routines. Every day, year after year: the same train to work, the same evening activities, the same holiday destinations. Some even eat the same dinner every night. Impulsivity is not high on the list of the attributes of the men in this book. But it may well be the attitude needed to perform to the utmost of one's powers in a changing world.

Again, traders are the odd ones out. The most obvious area is probably in their weakness for extravagance. For traders, it is more the rule than the exception to spend their wealth, preferably in as conspicuous a manner as possible, while value investors seem to prefer a more restrained approach to their money.

What unites all investors, however, is self-control and discipline. They are not swept along by emotional investments. They separate the facts and analyses from the expectations and hopes.

JESSE! JESSE! JESSE!

So, who is the best investor? Making the choice is something of a challenge, and a time-consuming one at that. In order to be fair, one must adjust for leverage, risk, tax, and not least the size of the assets under management. To complicate things further, there are some investors whose income is not known for certain. And how to deal with investors who started out with borrowed money? Their return is, by definition, infinite.

Despite the metrological problems, I had a stab at ranking the top five investors based on long-term returns. In the table below I have calculated what one dollar's worth of initial capital would be worth given their historical returns. To make it more comparable, I only included the investors who have managed listed assets. The result is surprising, to say the least.

Best investors	Annual returns	Number of years	$1 would have become
Jesse Livermore	55%	37 (1892–1929)	$11,022,315
Rakesh Jhunjhunwala	78%	26 (1985–)	$10,517,862
László Szombatfalvy	30%	46 (1965–2011)	$174, 339
Robert W. Wilson	30%	37 (1949–1986)	$16,809
Shelby Davis	23%	47 (1947–1994)	$16,440

Calculated on Jesse Livermore's wealth after 1929, but before he became ill with depression. László Szombatfalvy's returns are calculated on a capital of $1,000, instead of the borrowed money that was actually the case.

Turning one dollar into more than eleven million in 37 years is phenomenal. With abilities like that, it is understandable that Livermore in his youth was banned from most of America's bucket shops because he won all the time and more or less broke the banks. Livermore earned himself the epithet 'The world's greatest stock trader'. He is also a worthy candidate for 'The world's best investor'. Even if Carlos Slim, currently the world's richest man, was included in this ranking, he still couldn't touch Livermore. Unlike Livermore, Slim was born rich.

All the three major continents are represented in the table: America's best (Livermore), Asia's best (Jhunjhunwala), and Europe's best (Szombatfalvy). One objection to this particular ranking is that all of them started out with nothing – it's always easier to recoup a smaller sum than a large. On the other hand, I have not adjusted for expenses and extravagances along the way. Jesse Livermore was known for his ostentatious lifestyle, and his three divorces must have left quite a dent in his wallet.

It is worth noting that all five investors in the table managed their own capital. The stock market was very much their province. Two of the investors were typical traders (Livermore and Wilson), while the other three are best understood as value investors. Pole position goes to the investors who occasionally leveraged their assets to the fullest, something synonymous with higher risk.

Unless Rakesh Jhunjhunwala starts losing hand over fist or decides to retire, he will soon top the rankings. He is only 52 years old.

It is easier and less controversial to compare investors who have been managing public funds, even if this too has its metrological problems. If an investor changes fund mid-career, it can affect his ranking here. My aim has been to measure returns before fees, but for some investors no gross yield is available and I've had to make do with the net gain. Again, I have calculated what one dollar's worth of initial capital would ultimately have been worth.

Best public investors	Annual returns	Number of years	$1 would have become
George Soros	32%	31 (1969–2000)	5,468
Warren Buffett	20%	47 (1964–)	5,266
Walter J. Schloss	21%	44 (1955–2000)	3,048
James H. Simons	38%	23 (1988–2010)	1,649
Philip Carret	13%	55 (1928–1983)	1,348

All returns are net of fees except for Walter Schloss.

Compared with Livermore's feat of turning one dollar into eleven million, these seem modest results. But then you have to consider the size of the assets under management. Buffett, for example, has $100 billion in play. When Soros retired, his Quantum hedge fund had assets well over $10 billion. Simons managed even more. To succeed like Soros in turning $1 into almost $5,500 in the course of 31 years in the spotlight, and with billions to manage, is quite a feat.

If Buffett continues hale and hearty, he'll soon be number one. None of the others in this table remain active. Both Carret and Schloss have died, and Soros and Simons have retired.

Here too it is the value investors who dominate, but pride of place goes to a trader – or a short-term speculator as Soros himself likes to call himself. Simons in current fourth place is the most successful quantitative investor the world has ever seen.

BE CAUTIOUS

Although the investors' strategies and advice are mostly timeless, there is reason to be cautious. History may have a way of repeating itself, but sometimes it takes new paths. Don't make the mistake of thinking that because a model has proved itself in the past, it will continue to do so in the future. Investors' historical returns mask the fact that the fluctuations along the way were large and frequent. The fact that some financial gurus have at some point been ruined, or as near as, makes no difference (Jesse Livermore, Jim Slater, and others). And not at the beginning of their careers, either.

Even an experienced investor like George Soros lost his way when faced by the dot-com bubble. That false step saw his fund more than halved. The Canadian investor Preem Watsa, known as 'the Warren Buffett of Canada', invested in Greek bonds in 2011. Even Warren Buffett himself has got things wrong in his time, including investments in airlines and newspaper companies, where he failed to recognize looming structural changes.

It is hardly surprising that many of the older investors avoid borrowing and advocate having significant cash reserves.

Despite their long experience, quite a few investors came unstuck before they decided to retire. Among their number is Michael Steinhardt, who had run an extremely successful hedge fund for 22 years before he started investing abroad and lost nearly a third of the fund's value. Charlie Munger lost more than half the value of his partnership in 1973–4, which was significantly worse than the benchmark, before he stopped in 1975.

Ironically, there are investors whose analysis was correct, but were forced to throw in the towel because their timing was wrong. Julian Robertson, who for a while ran the largest and at times most successful hedge fund in the world, avoided investing in technology stocks throughout the 1990s. Right idea, wrong time. Weak returns caused him to bail out in March 2000, the same month that the dot-com bubble burst.

Some of the investors' counsel over the years has become obsolete because the market has changed. Many times it was a question of a once unique investment idea becoming so widespread that opportunities dried up. Philip Fisher, for example, never bought into a company if the price–earnings to growth ratio was higher than half the growth (PEG <0.5). At the time of writing it is hard to find any company that has such a low valuation. Those who are tempted to try to repeat Ed Seykota's and Michael Marcus' feats using trend-following strategies will find that the market is behaving differently now.

Times and conditions change. Sometimes this is barely noticeable, but still, it's there. When Warren Buffett recently advertised for his successor, he said, 'This person will need to be able to imagine things that have never happened before. I think that's very, very important.' It is easy to agree with him. A quarter of a century ago, few believed that China would become the largest country in terms of economic strength. Meanwhile, the entire financial system and the global economy are more fragile than perhaps ever before. The speed of economic change has never been greater. Companies on the S&P500 (a US index of the 500 largest companies) are replaced at a rate that was unimaginable a few decades ago. And very likely it will be even faster in future.

Despite these caveats, I am confident that the findings presented in this book will help current and future investors. The star fund managers together have more than 3,000 years of experience. And they are the best investors in the world – representing a veritable smorgasbord of different strategies, cultures, and circumstances. For a Westerner, it is fascinating to see how the Japanese stock market investor Shuhei Abe acted to survive 25 years of falling stock prices in Japan.

And do not be ashamed to take a leaf out of their book. In the investment world, it's the finest compliment. And for those who want to live and learn like the men in this book, there is every opportunity, as almost a third of the investors (30 of 99) have written books about their exploits in the financial markets. Many are seasoned with advice about life in general, an aspect not to be missed. Some of the books are even more interesting from a philosophical perspective than a financial one.

SIMPLEST IS BEST

If you still feel disoriented, you can always fall back on the wise words of the late Walter Schloss: 'If you are honest, hardworking, and reasonably intelligent and have good common sense, you can do well in the investment field as long as you are not too greedy and don't get too emotional when things go against you.'

The beauty of most of the advice in this book is its very simplicity – a good starting-point in becoming a good investor. It is underrated, or as Albert Einstein once said, 'Simplicity is the highest form of intellect.'

By far the most frequent recommendation is to invest only in what you understand. Successful investors have usually identified the areas where they show particular aptitude. They are not tempted to explore unknown territory, but instead focus on using their comparative advantages. Stay focused, stay sharp. Find out what type of investor you are, think about what you're good at, and then stick to it.

T. Boone Pickens is an oil and energy man, Ian Henderson's field is commodities, Mark Mobius: emerging markets, Ralph Wanger: fast-growing small-caps, and so on. You will find no investor in this book who has mastered all the disciplines. It is their focus and application that has borne fruit, don't forget.

Another frequent piece of advice is to think independently. Wise advice, yes, but probably easier said than done if you are a brand-new graduate taking her first hesitant steps as an investor. Things are rather different if your name is Warren Buffett and have 60 years of successful investments under your belt.

With experience comes resilience. Perseverance, however, is something best had from the outset. Remember that many successful investors began their careers with a humiliating crash. If you were to give up the first time an investment went west or you had a bad day, then your career as an investor would be a brief one. As an investor it is virtually impossible to be right all the time about all the right things. To succeed, you must put up with being wrong occasionally.

If you have invested poorly on the basis of incorrect analysis, but have learned from your mistakes, you probably have good grounds to hope for future success. Do not ignore your mistakes; see them as a step to the eternal learning process. The actress Ingrid Bergman once said that happiness is good health and a bad memory. To be a successful investor, you'll need good health and a good memory.

In this book I have tried to give a fair picture of intelligent, honest, and disciplined, but not inflexible, individuals – normal people who work hard. In all honesty, most of them are anything but ordinary. Read their biographies and you'll find many quirks of character.

Yet no matter how they look or behave, they are better than others at predicting the future, which is what it's all about. The financial system is a way to use future profits now to improve general welfare and make the market economy more efficient.

By way of conclusion, I want to share with you the advice that helped me most over the years. It comes from the American John D. Rockefeller, the richest person the world has ever seen: 'Tops and bottoms are only for fools.'

SHUHEI
ABE
JAPAN

ANNUAL YIELD
7.8%
for **14** YEARS
BENCHMARK -2.7%

I believe that the most important thing is to understand what you're good at. There are many legendary investors who have experienced remarkable success. In my opinion, each of these investors has had their own unique way of understanding and simplifying the complexity of their environment. Except for the first few years, I have been investing in a declining market for more than two decades. I survived because I stuck to the areas that I feel I understand. Despite extreme pessimism, there have always been opportunities where I could arbitrage the value gap. When price is excessively below a firm's value, you can still make money even in the worst of market environments.

My first principle is that no one can correctly predict the future. Therefore, when you evaluate potential investments, your thinking model should be simple. The variables that you consider in your model should not be too many. In the end, trying to predict something you cannot know is like throwing a dart in the dark. The foundation for your investment decision should therefore be based on what you can see and what you can hear.

When evaluating a potential investment, I look at three variables. First, I consider the sustainability of the firm's business model. Any business can be described by a simple equation, or sales less expenses. As an example, when analysing a firm's future sales, growth is defined by whether the unit price can be increased and more units can be sold. Secondly, it is important to evaluate the general industry outlook and its potential size to determine the company's edge and ability to maintain its profit margin. Naturally, a strong company in a growing market would make an attractive investment candidate, but in Japan, I have observed cases where a company is still able to grow in a shrinking market. And finally, who is the person that decides the future course of the firm. Is he or she trustworthy? Is he or she creative and innovative? Does he or she have a track record or the potential to build a scalable business? Focusing on these three variables alone, I believe you are able to identify whether the company has a real edge or not. In my view, this approach makes it easier to make an investment decision rather than trying to consider all potential variables.

BORN Sapporo, Japan, 1954.

EDUCATION Abe graduated in economics from Sophia University in Tokyo, followed by an MBA from Babson College in the US in 1982. He completed Harvard Business School's Advanced Management Program in 2005.

CAREER Abe began his career as an analyst for the Nomura Research Institute (Japan). He continued with three years in Japanese equity sales for Nomura Securities International in New York. Aged 31 he formed Abe Capital Research in 1985, where he managed Japanese equity investments for American and European investors. Four years later he founded the Tokyo-based SPARX Group. Abe continues to lead the SPARX Group as chairman and CEO.

INVESTMENT PHILOSOPHY Abe is a value investor, but likes to focus on evaluating the industry and business models. In addition he spends a great deal of time assessing company management. He is said to have an aggressive investment style, taking large stakes in companies and then working with management to enhance the value of their firms. This approach – relationship investing – includes teaming up with strategic operating partners to help companies realize their full potential. He is regarded as an activist.

OTHER He is said to be a disciple of George Soros, whom he has worked for. Abe was one of the first hedge-fund managers in Japan. SPARX Group is also the first independent, publicly traded investment firm in Japan, with approximately $7 billion in assets under management and offices in Hong Kong and Seoul. From being a Japanese equities small-cap boutique he has transformed the company into one of Asia's largest alternative investment firms. He is a guitar player and painter in his spare time.

Sources: Shuhei Abe; SPARX Asset Management; Wikipedia.

CHARLES T.
AKRE
USA

ANNUAL YIELD
14.1%
for **22** YEARS
BENCHMARK 8.2%

The best investments are those which we refer to as 'compounding machines'. Our process is guided by the framework we call the 'three-legged stool.' The first leg we describe as the business model, helping us to identify businesses which have enduring high returns on capital and pricing power in excess of input cost. The second leg we call the people model. This helps us identify managers who operate in the best interests of all shareholders. The third leg we call the reinvestment model. This allows us to identify those businesses with extensive reinvestment opportunities combined with a history of disciplined reinvestment results. When we identify one of these 'compounding machines' we are stingy with the purchase price, knowing that our compound rate of return will be substantially affected by our starting valuation.

Take nothing for granted! Constantly revisit all your assumptions and conclusions hoping to discover where you might be wrong. 'It's not what we don't know that kills us; it's what we know that ain't so.' Constantly study and prepare.

The value is in the journey! Treat all you encounter with respect and dignity, as people matter more than either businesses or profits!

BORN Washington DC, USA 1943.

EDUCATION He recieved a BA in English Literature from the American University, Washington, DC in 1968.

CAREER Akre began his career with 21 years at the investment firm Johnston, Lemon & Co. where he was head of research and of the asset management division as well as being a shareholder and director. At the age of 46 he left and established Akre Capital Management (ACM) in 1989 and serves as managing member, chief executive officer, and chief investment officer.

INVESTMENT PHILOSOPHY Akre is a bottom-up value–growth stock investor. He seeks companies with high, sustainable, predictable returns on equity and promising reinvestment options at times when stock prices do not adequately reflect either. His favoured valuation metric is price to free cash flow, but he requires the company to have at least 15 % returns on equity. When investing he is looking for stock price appreciation from both earnings growth and a revaluation of the company's P/E ratio based on increased investor confidence. It is a buy-and-hold strategy with low turnover. The portfolio is usually concentrated to fewer than 20 positions, which he holds for a long period. He regards market volatility as a powerful opportunity and spends little time with Excel spreadsheets. According to him, the greatest mistake you can make as an investor is to buy an expensive stock whose price is based upon its historical record of growth.

OTHER ACM's hedge fund has produced performance of 15 % compounded for eighteen years compared with 8 % compounded performance for S&P500 since 1993. Its headquarters are in Middleburg, Virginia, a town with one traffic light. When Akre holds presentations he habitually asks a rhetorical question: 'What is the value of a penny if it doubles every day for 30 days?' The answer is $10.7 million!

Sources: Charles T. Akre; Akre Capital Management, LCC; SMA Composite; Morningstar Wikipedia.

FABIO
ALPEROWITCH
BRAZIL

ANNUAL YIELD
34%
for **19** YEARS
BENCHMARK 14%

Never believe anyone. People are naturally biased. So you must be convinced yourself before making any investment. For this, you have to double-check (or triple-check) all information with multiple sources. When visiting a company, for example, interviewing the CEO or the CFO will lead you to biased conclusions (I have never heard a CEO say that the business is bad, the company is poorly managed, sales will fall in the long term, and margins will shrink). It is key to talk to the middle management, suppliers, blue-collar workers, main clients, ex-employees, and industry experts (but never sell-side analysts). Without this thorough process, you will see only part of the picture, and you will probably make bad investments. It is not easy; it takes time. But the results pay off.

Stay close to the real world. You will never make good investments from your office just sitting behind the computer. Get out there, visit supermarkets, interview people in the street, visit malls, fairs, etc. Travel a lot. Despite the fact that our fund invests solely in Brazil, during the past three years we have visited China six times, as well India, Chile, Mexico, the US,

Germany, the UK, Russia, and may other places, just to do research. Competition may come from anywhere. New managerial skills could be learned in different companies from different sectors. Open your mind. You have to be focused, but if you narrow your expertise too much perhaps you'll end up a good executive in that sector and not a good investor. Streets have more lessons to be learned than classrooms.

Value creation/destruction. A good company run by good people may create value over time. An Excel spreadsheet will never translate the real value of a company, because no analyst in the world is able to predict what a company is going to make within 5 years (not to mention in perpetuity). All the target prices are wrong. All the spreadsheets and forecasts are wrong as well. So, the qualitative analysis of the business and people is by far more important than the quantitative one. Good management creates value over time: launch new products, enter in new businesses and new geographies, make good acquisitions, bring on good people, and so on and so forth. On the other hand, bad people destroy value. Never buy a company just because it is a bargain. Cheap could become even cheaper. Select the businesses to invest in for the qualitative aspects, and just check whether you are not paying up front for value creation, by understanding what the share price is embedding in terms of expectations. Invest for the long run (our average holding period is 10 years), but revisit the case and the valuation very often (every quarter at least).

BORN Sao Paulo, Brazil 1971.

EDUCATION He holds a degree in Business Administration from Fundação Getúlio Vargas (FGV-SP).

CAREER After three years at Proctor&Gamble he founded FAMA Investimentos 1993 when only 22 years old. He is responsible for portfolio management and research.

INVESTMENT PHILOSOPHY Alperowitch is a small-cap stock market investor. He uses fundamental research to identify high quality companies to own for a decade or so. Because he concentrates on smaller companies in the early stages of growth, their products, markets, and company leadership are more important than the raw figures. Alperowitch also takes an active part in running the companies, and usually sits on the board.

OTHER Alperowitch manages around $1 billion. Even accounting in dollars (+31%) the result is stunning. One of FAMA's internal polices is not to speak with other fund managers or to read sell-side reports. In his free time he is interested in fine wines, astrophotography, and triathlons.

Sources: Fabio Alperowitch; FAMA Investimentos.

KIEKIE
BOENAWAN
INDONESIA

ANNUAL YIELD

26.4%

for **14** YEARS

BENCHMARK 11%

Investment is part science and part art. Some things can be studied intelligently, but others you have to learn through experience. These experiences come in the form of mistakes that you made in your investing journey. I have made a lot of mistakes during my career as an investment manager. Some of them I made repeatedly until I eventually learned from them. These mistakes are hard to learn from since sometimes they give you the initial impression, usually in the short term, that they are not mistakes at all. Some have caused me so much pain that I have learned never to repeat them again. One of the mistakes that I made quite often was investing in companies with a bad track record of corporate governance. There are a lot of companies, especially the small- and mid-cap companies with poor corporate governance in emerging economies. In the long term, these companies tend to be very bad investment for investors. They have poor transparency and treat public investors very badly. Most have dubious accounting practices, inflated earnings during share placements, and lots of transfer pricing and related party transactions that are not beneficial to the investing public. I have learned the hard way that capable management and trusted business partners are two extremely important factors in a successful business.

I also learned the hard way about black swan events. You often hear about it and you know that extraordinarily bad outcomes happen more often than you might think. However, you will never really understand the true meaning of this until you experience it yourself. In just a little over a decade, I have experienced two extremely unlikely events. One such event was during the Asian crisis, when my local currency plummeted from about 2,200 rupiah to the dollar to as much as 17,000 rupiah, an almost 90 per cent devaluation against the dollar in less than a year. The other one is the 2008 global crisis where the world stock markets went down on average about 50 % in a year. I would never expect that these events could happen but they did. It is one thing to be told about this black swan event but to experience it first hand is really a mind opener. The experience taught me to never underestimate the unexpected unlikely outcome.

Over the years, I also learned that it is better to be more cautious and be patient at the propect of an opportunity. I learned to be able to distinguish between what is a really great investment opportunity and a disguised good investment opportunity. It is difficult and unless you are honest towards yourself, you find it very hard to separate the truths from the illusions. In the long run, it is always rewarding to be more on the cautious side and be patient. Once an opportunity presents itself, you have to be aggressive in taking advantage of it.

BORN Bandung, Indonesia 1962.

EDUCATION Boenawan graduated in Computer Engineering in 1986 from Case Western Reserve University in Cleveland, Ohio. In 1988 he took an MBA in Finance at the same university.

CAREER Kiekie Boenawan started as an investment banker at Jardine Fleming in Indonesia. Aged 31 he founded PT Jardine Fleming Nusantara Investment Management where he was the investment director. Since 1999 he has been chief investment officer for Schroder Investment Management Indonesia.

INVESTMENT PHILOSOPHY Boenawan is an emerging markets investor in the stock market with Asia as his working area. One of the most important criteria is choosing capable management with a good corporate governance record since most of the companies are rather young in a sometimes unproven market. Boenawan believes that having a good business partner is the key to a successful investment. Another important factor is a true understanding of the nature of the business to be invested in. He regards himself as a growth investor and uses GARP (Growth AT Reasonable Price) as a key value parameter.

OTHER Boenawan has more than $5 billion of funds under management invested in Indonesia capital market. He became a CFA charterholder in 2000. In his spare time he likes to play tennis or go to the cinema with his family.

Sources: Kiekie Boenawan; Schroders; Schroders Dana Prestasi; Wikipedia.

JOHN C.
BOGLE
US

ANNUAL YIELD
17%
for **14** YEARS
BENCHMARK 13%

John Bogle's 'Five Rules of Investing' Balance opportunity and risk. Allocate your assets between stocks and bonds consistent with your wealth, your tolerance for risk, and your age. (Your percentage allocation to bonds should equal your age.)

Diversify, diversify, diversify. Owning a very large number of individual stocks and bonds has always been a good idea. However, in today's environment of financial failures, global competition, and technological innovation, maximum diversification is essential. ('Owning a total stock-market index fund and a total bond-market index fund is a sound strategy'.)

Focus on the long term. That is, be an investor who owns businesses, not a speculator who bets on stocks. In the short run, as Benjamin Graham has pointed out, the stock market is a voting machine, but in the long run it is a weighing machine.

Minimize the costs of investing. The beauty of indexing is not only that the diversification it offers is priceless, but also that it is price-less. The management fees and expenses, sales loads, and hidden portfolio transaction costs of the typical actively managed mutual fund come to about 2 per cent per year. Over, say a fifty-year investment lifetime, these costs will consume about 75 per cent of your capital. The miracle of compounding returns can be overwhelmed by the tyranny of compounding costs.

Stay the course. The temptations to get out of the market (usually when it's gone way down) and to pile in (usually when it's setting new highs) are overwhelming, and clearly counterproductive. Do your best to follow these proven principles through the inevitable swings in the economy and financial markets, and do your best not to peek at your portfolio. When you build it over your career, and see what it's worth when the time comes to draw down some of it when you retire, you'll be amazed at how much wealth you've accumulated.

BORN Montclair, New Jersey, USA 1929.

EDUCATION Bogle graduated from Princeton University in Economics in 1951.

CAREER He began in the mutual-fund industry at Wellington Management. Aged 45 he founded the Vanguard Group, Inc., where he served as chairman and chief executive officer until 1996 and senior chairman until 2000.

INVESTMENT PHILOSOPHY John Bogle is unusual in this gathering, for his strategy is not to beat the market, but rather to lose as little as possible when compared to it. He is the creator of the index-funds phenomenon and is obsessed with low cost management and diversification. His lifelong crusade is against fund managers who charge high fees and provide mediocre returns. His quote 'What's the point of looking for the needle in the haystack? Why not own the haystack' explains his view on stock picking. In addition, Bogle has several other cornerstones in his investment strategy. One is to never underrate the importance of asset allocation and always have 'dry powder' in the portfolios. Another crucial point is to be wary of forecasts and even to neglect strategists. He is also sceptical of mutual funds with superior performance records; they often falter in the end and chasing past performance is all too often a loser's game.

OTHER Bogle offered the first index fund in 1974 and Vanguard has now become the largest mutual fund in the world, with 160 mutual funds and almost $2 trillion in assets under management. He has written nine books, the latest, Don't Count On It! Reflections on Investment Illusions, Capitalism, 'Mutual' Funds, Indexing, Entrepreneurship, Idealism, and Heroes published when Bogle celebrated his 81st birthday. In 1999, Fortune named him as one of the investment industry's four 'Giants of the Twentieth Century' and five years later Time named Bogle as one of the world's hundred most powerful and influential people.

....

Sources: John C. Bogle; John C. Bogle, *Bogle on Mutual Funds: New Perspectives for the Intelligent Investor* (1993), John C. Bogle, *The Little Book of Common Sense Investing* (2007), Vanguard Funds; Vanguard's Total Market Index Fund.

ANTHONY BOLTON
UK

ANNUAL YIELD
19.5%
for **28** YEARS
BENCHMARK 13.5%

→ Invest in businesses you understand, with good franchises run by management you trust.
→ Highly geared companies can be rewarding, but they are the most risky.
→ To be a good investor, having the right temperament and being happy to go against the crowd are more important than having a very high IQ.

BORN London, UK 1950.

EDUCATION Bolton received an MA in Engineering and Business Studies from the University of Cambridge in 1971.

CAREER Bolton began his career in the City as a graduate trainee at Keyser Ullman in 1971. Five years later he moved to Schlesinger's, where he became an investment manager. In 1979, he was recruited by Fidelity Investment Management as one of its first London-based investment managers. Bolton retired from full-time investment management at the end of 2007, but he continued to work at Fidelity as a mentor and remained involved in Fidelity's investment process. In 2009, he announced his decision to return to managing money, and relocated to Hong Kong in 2010 to manage the Fidelity China Special Situations Fund.

INVESTMENT PHILOSOPHY Bolton is a value investor with his sole focus on the stock market. Even if Bolton regards himself as a contrarian, he is more flexible than most. He puts a lot of effort into identifying turnaround candidates – with considerable success. He also prefers companies with an M&A angle, and uses technical analysis to crosscheck the fundamental view. But the cornerstones in his investment approach are that value stocks outperform growth stocks in the long run, and that unpopular, cheap stocks give the best return. He is careful with financially geared companies, as that is where by his own admission he has incurred the largest historic losses. Bolton compares the present valuation with the historic average to get a sense of the value. The strength of the franchise and management are other crucial issues in his bottom-up analysis. His investments are always preceded by a visit to the company. Overall, Bolton uses a very time-consuming, close, and strict investment style; hard work is his middle name.

OTHER Between 1979 and 2007, he outperformed the stockmarket by six percentage points a year on average, a better return than any competitor over the same period. According to a former colleague, Peter Lynch, Bolton also has steady nerves and good judgement. He has been nicknamed the 'British Buffet'. He has written two books and his hobby is composing classical music. His compositions have been performed at St Paul's Cathedral in London.

....

Sources: Anthony Bolton; Anthony Bolton, Investing against the tide (2007); Fidelity Special Situations Fund; Wikipedia.

SIR RON BRIERLEY

NEW ZEALAND

ANNUAL YIELD

15.5%

for **20** YEARS

BENCHMARK 10%

A ny success I have had as an investor is entirely due to research. Knowledge is power! I research a company file in strict chronological sequence, going back years or decades if available. An Annual Report from the Fifties or Sixties may seem of little relevance to today's market, but the historical data helps to create a sixth sense regarding the company which finally emerges in the present. Knowledge of the industry and of other companies in the same market is also important.

Own a share of a business, not a speculative piece of paper. If you buy one share at one price, would you wish, in theory at least, to buy all of the shares at that price?

As Warren Buffett says, don't invest in anything you don't understand.

I look for hard assets, no excess debt, and I steer away from technology and personal service businesses.

Put all your eggs in one basket! That is the opposite of accepted investment wisdom—which will protect against wipeout, but never produce better than average results. Back your own judgement to score the big wins.

There are no shortcuts to success, no magic formula, and you never stop learning.

BORN Wellington, New Zealand 1937.

EDUCATION Sir Ron dropped out of a part-time course in Accountancy at Victoria University of Wellington.

CAREER Having been a clerk and having managed two smaller ventures, Sir Ron started Brierley Investment Ltd. (BIL) aged 24 with no capital. By 1984, BIL was the largest company in New Zealand by market capitalization, and in 1987 it had stakes in over 300 companies. After suffering in the 1987 stock market crash, in 1990 he moved his focus to the Guinness Peat Group. He officially retired 2001, but is still active as a board member and in the stock market. His latest corporate vehicle is Mercantile Investment Co. Ltd.

INVESTMENT PHILOSOPHY Value investor and corporate raider is the best description of Sir Ron's investment style. He trades in stock exchange shares with a view to short- and medium-term appreciation and to taking over or acquiring substantial holdings in companies in order ultimately to participate in management and the reorganization of their finances. He searches the share market for the weak and vulnerable, looking for investment opportunities in underperforming or poorly managed companies – but only undervalued asset-rich companies. 'We challenge companies, we challenge concepts, we put forward proposals, and not all of them are universally accepted', as one of his colleagues put it. He also looks for opportunities with companies that could be stripped of underperforming divisions or assets where remaining assets could be regenerated (hence his reputation as an asset stripper). He has had a broad range of investments, from the Paris department store Galeries Lafayette to Air New Zealand.

OTHER Sir Ron is known as a brilliant analyst. He is famous for his head for business and his ability to work many days in a row. He is one of the richest people in New Zealand and is a stamp collector.

Sources: Sir Ron Brierley; The Dominion Post, 2008; Fairfax Digital, 2002; Wikipedia.

WARREN
BUFFETT
USA

ANNUAL YIELD
19.8%
for **47** YEARS
BENCHMARK 9.2%

To invest successfully over a lifetime does not require a stratospheric IQ, unusual business insights, or inside information. What's needed is a sound intellectual framework for making decisions and to keep emotions from corroding that framework.

Charlie and I avoid businesses whose futures we can't evaluate, no matter how exciting their products may be. In the past, it required no brilliance for people to foresee the fabulous growth that awaited such industries as autos (in 1910), aircraft (in 1930), and television sets (in 1950). But the future then also included competitive dynamics that would decimate almost all of the companies entering those industries.

Even the survivors tended to come away bleeding.

There have been three primary causes for why investors didn't earn juicy returns despite a multi-decade bull market: first, high costs, usually because investors traded excessively or spent far too much on investment management; second, portfolio decisions based on tips and fads rather than on thoughtful, quantified evaluation of businesses; and third, a start-and-stop approach to the market (marked by untimely entries after an advance has been long under way) and exits (after periods of stagnation or decline). Investors should remember that excitement and expenses are their enemies.

BORN Omaha, Nebraska USA 1930.

EDUCATION Buffett graduated with a B.Sc. in Business Administration at the University of Nebraska–Lincoln and took an MBA at Columbia Business School; he also attended the New York Institute of Finance.

CAREER Warren Buffett started off as an investment salesman at his father's firm Buffett-Falk & Co. After three years he was employed by his old professor Benjamin Graham at Graham-Newman Corp as a security analyst. When Graham closed the business in1956 Buffett started on his own, Buffett Partnership Ltd. Aged 34 he gained control over Berkshire Hathaway where he still serves as chairman and CEO.

INVESTMENT PHILOSOPHY Buffett is the most famous and successful disciple of Benjamin Graham's value investment philosophy. But he has modernized the strategy, which was once only quantitative, by incorporating far more qualitative factors, things you cannot get from the balance sheet. Buffett sets out to acquire major companies trading at a discount to their intrinsic value, and to hold onto them for a long time. If the company is wholly owned he rarely considers selling it on. He will only invest in businesses that he understands, run by honest and competent people, and he always insists on a margin of safety. The insurance business has been his biggest focus so far.

Buffett is obsessed with the idea of compounding growth; unlike Graham, he believes a discount of 50 % to intrinsic value is insufficient. Therefore he likes to figure out a business's major strengths and weaknesses so he is comfortable that the business will continue to create value, not just over the next quarter, but over the next five or ten years. Returns on capital and cash flow are more important metrics for Buffett than earnings per share. He is first and foremost a big cash generator. Technical analyses, macroeconomics, or investments through derivatives are not given much importance or are avoided altogether. The portfolio is concentrated; by mid-2012 it comprised only ten larger listed positions. Including the unlisted businesses, Berkshire Hathaway owns over 50 companies. The portfolio is considerably more sophisticated than just a load of long-term share purchases. For example, as of mid-2012 it included sell options on the share index for $8.5 billion.

Buffett has repeatedly stated that his simple willingness to 'think independently' is the key to investment success. The most striking thing about Buffett is that he is utterly confident in his ability to judge the value of a company and that, in the end, the market will recognize that he is right.

OTHER He started playing a game of stock marketing with one of his sisters when he was eleven, and his favourite toy was a coin counter. He is nicknamed the 'Wizard of Omaha' and runs an empire with $185 billion in capital from a small office with 23 employees. Forbes estimated his wealth to be $44 billion in 2012, which makes him the third richest person in the world. Buffett is also a notable philanthropist, having pledged to give away 99 % of his fortune in the largest act of charitable giving in the world's history. He plays bridge and the ukulele.

Sources: Benjamin Graham, *The Intelligent Investor* (1949); Robert P. Miles, *The Warren Buffett CEO – Secrets from the Berkshire Hathaway Managers* (2002); Alice Schroeder, *The Snowball – Warren Buffett and the business of life* (2008); Berkshire Hathaway chairman's letter, 2004; Letter to Berkshire Hathaway shareholders, September 2009; Wikipedia.

EDOUARD
CARMIGNAC
FRANCE

ANNUAL YIELD
11%
for **23** YEARS
BENCHMARK 3%

A nticipate and never take anything for granted. Never ignore the market, but rely on the real economy. The market at best will make you proud, but it's the real economy that will make you win.

Creativity requires a free mindset. Independence remains, and will remain, the basis of Carmignac Gestion's business model. Freedom also goes with self-discipline. Being daring and sticking to one's convictions are the only ways to generate value in the long run. Keep digging until you reach your own conviction. Because if you don't buy on strong, well thought-out convictions, you'll sell poorly.

Work, work, work.

BORN Paris, France 1947.

EDUCATION Edouard Carmignac holds a degree in Economics from the University of Paris (1969) and a MBA from Columbia University (1972).

CAREER Carmignac started as an analyst at Blyth Eastern Dillon in New York in 1972. Three years later he moved on to Paribas, where he worked with international financial transactions. In 1976, he was appointed assistant director at Banque de la Société Financière Européenne responsible for loans to the energy and mining sectors. He worked as a stockbroker at Hamant-Carmignac in 1984–89. He founded Carmignac Gestion in 1989, and, in his capacity as chairman, is closely involved in the management strategy of its UCITS funds.

INVESTMENT PHILOSOPHY Carmignac uses a 'top-down' investment strategy. He looks for sustained economic trends, and then concentrates his investments in sectors and companies that stand to benefit from them and normally has no more than 50 positions. He also uses simple and liquid derivatives on indices to hedge portfolios in difficult times and changes gear quickly in rebounds. His can be described as opportunistic, non-trend-following style with focus on safeguarding capital. Carmignac invests in all asset classes all over the world but emerging markets make up for more than half of his assets. He has a streak of the contrarian in him. One of his moves that created great attention was to go against the stock market before it de facto turned.

OTHER With over €45 billion of assets under management, Carmignac Gestion is one of the leading asset managers in Europe. Almost half of the equity investments are in emerging markets. Two giant Warhol portraits of Lenin and Mao flanking his desk are there to remind him that nothing should ever be taken for granted. Recently he funded an advertising campaign in France in which he strongly objected to proposed laws to reduce the retirement age to 60 while taxing the highest salaries at a rate of 75 %.

Sources: Edouard Carmignac; Carmignac Gestion; Wikipedia.

PHILIP
CARRET
USA

ANNUAL YIELD
13%
for **55** YEARS
BENCHMARK 3%

Philip Carret's twelve commandments for speculators:
→ Never hold fewer than ten different securities covering five different fields of business.
→ At least once every six months reappraise every security held.
→ Keep at least half the total fund in income-producing securities.
→ Consider yield the least important factor in analysing any stock.
→ Be quick to take losses, reluctant to take profits.
→ Never put more than 25 % of a given fund into securities about which detailed information is not readily and regularly available.
→ Avoid 'inside information' like the plague.
→ Seek facts diligently; advice never.
→ Ignore mechanical formulas [such as price–earnings ratios] for valuing securities.
→ When stocks are high, money rates rising, and business prosperous, at least half a given fund should be placed in short-term bonds.
→ Borrow money sparingly and only when stocks are low, money rates low or falling, and business depressed.
→ Set aside a moderate proportion of available funds for the purchase of long-term options on stocks of promising companies whenever available.

BORN Lynn, Massachusetts, USA 1896. Died 1998.

EDUCATION He graduated from Harvard College and spent one year at business school.

CAREER Carret first spent a couple of years working in the financial industry. Then, while a reporter and feature writer for the financial magazine Barron's he began managing money for family and friends in 1924. He went on to establish what evolved into the Pioneer Fund in 1928. Later he founded Carret Zane Capital in 1962. He kept managing the fund until 1983, aged 87.

INVESTMENT PHILOSOPHY The title of one of his books, *The Art of Speculation*, gives the false image of a short-term trader. Carret was the opposite, being the first famous value investor. He did his own research, analysed data, and only invested in a company if its stock price did not reflect the company's real value, and if he saw potential for growth. His remark 'There is no substitute for buying quality assets and allowing them to compound over the long term. Patience can produce uncommon profits' described his main objective. Small over-the-counter stocks represented a substantial part of his portfolio and he preferred to buy semi listed stocks, which were not so often subject to course manipulation. A strong balance sheet was a crucial prerequisite for investment. He believed that options were useful when the market was bad, and as a rule he even kept cash available just for that. Leverage was used only when the market was low and there was extreme fear. He was mainly a stock market investor, but also used the bond market from time to time. He regarded the footnotes appended to annual reports as the most useful source of information.

OTHER Carret is famous for having the longest history of investing. His had 55 excellent compounded gain years as a fund manager despite major depressions, recessions, and world war. He founded the Pioneer Fund six years before Benjamin Graham first published Security Analysis. He was said to be a voracious reader. Warren Buffett and Carret exchanged ideas on a regular base for several years. At the 1996 Berkshire Hathaway Annual Meeting, Warren Buffett said: 'The main thing is to find wonderful businesses, like Phil Carret, who's here today, always did. He's one of my heroes, and that's an approach he's used. If you've never met Phil, don't miss the opportunity. You'll learn more talking with him for fifteen minutes than by listening to me here all day.' Carret wrote two books and continued to work on Wall Street even after he had turned a hundred. He was an avid chaser of eclipses and travelled the world to view them. His grandfather had been Napoleon's paymaster general.

Sources: Philip Carret's twelve commandments for speculators; Pioneer Fund; Pioneer Investment; Wikipedia.

LEE
COOPERMAN
USA

ANNUAL YIELD
14%
for **20** YEARS
BENCHMARK 6.9%

→ Stick to your sphere of competence. If you don't understand the investment don't make it.

→ As Warren Buffett has observed, in your investment lifetime the number of great ideas you will have are limited. When you recognize one, concentrate prudently.

→ If an investment sounds too good to be true, it probably isn't. Generally I am an advocate of the notion that hard work never killed anyone and full engagement and focus will pay off in the long run, assuming you also have a good dose of good luck.

BORN South Bronx, New York USA 1943.

EDUCATION Cooperman received his undergraduate degree from Hunter College and his MBA from Columbia University.

CAREER After a short period as a quality control engineer at Xerox before he took his MBA, Cooperman joined Goldman Sachs, where he spent 22 years in the investment research department. In 1989, he became chairman and CEO of Goldman Sachs Asset Management and was chief investment officer of the equity product line, including managing the GS Capital Growth Fund. In 1991, aged 48, he left to found Omega Advisors Inc., where he is chairman.

INVESTMENT PHILOSOPHY Cooperman is a diversified hedge-fund value investor. His management disciplines are as follows: market direction on the stock market both long and short; determine if the market is over- or undervalued; asset allocation, determining what asset class has the best prospective investment returns twelve months ahead; going from the basic level stocks vs. bonds vs. cash to more complex choices such as investment-grade vs. high yield bonds, and so on; finding undervalued individual stocks; finding overvalued stocks on the short side; and taking macro investments in currencies, global fixed income and the major international indices. The bread-and-butter business is the stock picking on the long side, and that is also where Cooperman has been most successful. He and his team seek companies trading at significant discounts to their private-market values, often due to inappropriately valued growth prospects: he basically searches for quality-growth companies.

OTHER Omega Advisors manages around $6 billion. When at Goldman Sachs, for nine consecutive years Cooperman was voted the number one portfolio strategist in the Institutional Investor All-America Research Team survey. Forbes estimated his wealth in 2011 to be $2.2 billion. He has taken 'The Giving Pledge', a campaign to encourage the wealthiest people in the US to commit to giving most of their money to philanthropic causes. In addition, he is involved in several charitable activities. Recently he published an open letter to President Barack Obama accusing him of waging class warfare.

Sources: Lee Cooperman; Omega Advisers; Wikipedia.

RAY
DALIO
USA

ANNUAL YIELD
13%
for **35** YEARS

BENCHMARK 8%

While most others seem to believe that mistakes are bad things, I believe mistakes are good things, because I believe that most learning comes via making mistakes and reflecting on them. Blaming bad outcomes on anyone or anything other than oneself is both incorrect and subversive to one's progress. It is incorrect because bad things come at everyone, and it is your challenge and test to successfully deal with whatever comes at you. Blaming bad outcomes on anyone or anything other than oneself is essentially wishing that reality were different than it is, which is silly. It is also subversive because it diverts one's attention away from mustering the personal strength and other qualities that are required if one is to produce the best possible outcomes. Remember, Nature is testing you, and it is not sympathetic.

Everyone has weaknesses. The main difference between unsuccessful and successful people is that unsuccessful people don't find and address them, and successful people do. That is why, as one of our managers has observed, reflective people are much more successful than deflective people.

In order to make money in the market you have to be an independent thinker. And, I think, creative too.

BORN Queens, New York USA 1949.

EDUCATION Dalio received a BA from Long Island University and an MBA from Harvard Business School in 1973.

CAREER Dalio worked on the floor of the New York Stock Exchange and invested in commodity futures. After his MBA, he started work as director of commodities at Dominick & Dominick LLC. In 1974, he became a futures trader and broker at Shearson Hayden Stone. In 1975, aged 26, he founded the investment management firm, Bridgewater Associates where he is president and mentor.

INVESTMENT PHILOSOPHY Dalio is a hedge fund investor with macro investments as his speciality. He is a master of the diversification needed to enable him to steer his giant funds. He bets mainly on economic trends, such as changes in exchange rates, inflation, and GDP growth round the globe. He spends most of his time trying to figure out how economic and financial events fit together in a coherent framework. Bond and currency markets, in which Dalio is an expert, are widely believed to represent the greatest bulk of profits historically. But he is also active in other asset classes. Gold was one of the company's largest contributors in 2010. In stocks Bridgewater tends to make relatively small, but numerous equities investments, sometimes having several hundred equity positions. He regards the consensus as 'often wrong', which is why he judges independent thinking to be the main criteria in managing money.

OTHER He is said to be intelligent and idiosyncratic, and manages the world's largest hedge fund with $120 billion in assets and 1,200 employees. In 2011, Bridgewater was ranked both the largest and the best-performing hedge-fund manager in the world, which is a unique combination. With its 35 billion profit in US dollars for clients Bridgewater has furthermore become the hedge fund with the highest yield ever in absolute figures. The last 18 years' performance is estimated to have been 15 % annually before fees. One of the more striking features of Bridgewater Associates is the corporate culture that Dalio has created. Dalio has presented the concept in a 123-page online book, *Principles*. He bought his first shares at the age of 12, and according to the New Yorker he had a net worth of US$10 billion as of 2011. Dalio is a practitioner of transcendental meditation; his main hobby is music – jazz, blues, and rock 'n' roll (his father was a jazz musician). Recently, he joined a philanthropic campaign, pledging to give away at least half of his money.

Sources: Ray Dalio, *Principles*; CNBC; Bridgewater Associates; gurufocus.com; The New Yorker, 2011; Wikipedia.

SHELBY C.
DAVIS
USA

ANNUAL YIELD
23%
for **47** YEARS
BENCHMARK 7%

→ You make most of your money in a bear market. You just don't realize it at the time.

→ Great companies bought at great prices should be like great friends—you do not want to drop them precipitously.

→ History provides a crucial insight regarding market crises: they are inevitable, painful, and ultimately surmountable.

BORN Peoria, Illinois, USA 1909. Died 1994.

EDUCATION Davis graduated from Princeton University and took a Master's at Columbia University in 1931. He earned a Ph.D. in political science at the Graduate Institute of International Studies, Geneva, in 1934.

CAREER His studies complete, he first worked at his brother-in-law's investment firm for five years before becoming a freelance writer. Aged 38 he got $50,000 in seed capital from his wife and founded Shelby Cullom Davis & Company, mainly to manage insurance stocks. Between 1969 and 1975 he was also US Ambassador to Switzerland.

INVESTMENT PHILOSOPHY Davis was a specialized stock market value investor. He only invested in companies he knew well and where he had an edge (insurance companies in most cases). He focused on fundamentals, and especially looked for a solid balance sheet making sure the insurer did not hold risky assets such as junk bonds. He then measured the management quality and made trips to meet with management and drill them. He searched for what he called 'compounding machines', but equally he liked a boost from earnings and from investors bidding up the multiple. The strategy was known as the 'Davis Double Play'. It was a buy-and-hold strategy, and he kept a long-term perspective through bull and bear markets. He was probably one of the first US investors abroad when he invested in Japanese insurance companies in the early 1960s. He recommended diversification, so that the ones you were wrong about were balanced by the ones you were right about.

OTHER By the time of his death in 1994, he had turned the original $50,000 stake into $900 million. In 47 years he had increased his stake 18.000 fold! The strategy of focusing on the insurance industry came to him after he had studied Benjamin Graham's writings. Davis made the Forbes 400 list in 1988, and other than Warren Buffett he was the only one to make the list by picking stocks for a living. He gave all his wealth to a charitable trust and was known for extreme frugality – instead of playing tennis with new balls he used old, ratty ones.

Sources: John Rothschild, The Davis Dynasty (2001); Investopedia; Wikipedia.

RICHARD H.
DRIEHAUS
USA

ANNUAL YIELD
20%
for **25** YEARS
BENCHMARK 5%

A stock's price is rarely the same as the company's value. Reason for that is the valuation process is flawed. Stock prices are heavily affected by market dynamics and by investors' emotions. These emotions swing widely from pessimism to optimism. Also, many investors buy stocks with the intention of holding them for several years based upon information that really only applies to a short-term time horizon. While the information they are using to invest may be valuable, it is often the wrong information for their investment timeframe. If people invest in a company based on current information, they have to be prepared to act on any changes to that information in a much shorter timeframe than most investors are prepared to do. So therefore I respond more readily to new information than other investors. Nevertheless, one has to constantly compare a stock's technical and fundamental earnings growth rate against other stocks that may not be in the portfolio, but that have even better technical and fundamental outlooks. It is interesting to note the 80:20 rule here: fewer than 20 % of my stocks have produced more than 80 % of my gains.

Often when I talk to consultants, they like to see a very systematic, value-based process. They think that each stock has to be submitted to some type of disciplined, precise, and uniform evaluation. But the real world is not that precise. I'm convinced there is no universal valuation method. In fact, in the short run, valuation is not the key factor. Each company's stock price is unique to that company's place in the market environment and to its own phase in its corporate development. We don't ignore value, but realize in the short-to-intermediate term it is not the determinant factor in a stock's price movement. It has been said in the short term, a stock's price is like a voting machine, but in the long term it's a weighing machine. Over a full market cycle, the daily price action of a stock is irrelevant to the longer-term worth of a company.

Most people believe high turnover is risky. Again, I think just the opposite. High turnover reduces risk when it is the result of taking a series of small losses in order to avoid larger losses. I don't hold on to stocks with deteriorating fundamentals or price patterns. For me, this kind of turnover makes sense. It reduces risk. More money can be made buying high and selling at even higher prices. I try to buy stocks that have already had good price moves, that are often making new highs, and that have positive relative strength. These are stocks in demand by other investors. The risk is that I'm buying near the top. But I would much rather be invested in a stock that is increasing in price and take the risk that it may begin to decline than invest in a stock that is already in a decline and try to guess when it will turn around. The above philosophy is most successful in a bull market. In bear markets, the largest gains may come from stocks that have declined the greatest percentage from their previous highs. Look for individual stocks with saucer bottoms or other technical indications that the stock is about to rebound. Another strategic approach is to buy a class of stocks and/or a specific sector (such as technology) in the bottom decile(s) from their former peaks. Some of the best opportunities may be in stocks recovering from a significant market decline. For example, in the short-to-intermediate term, tech stocks that have been oversold have doubled in just one quarter from a major bottom. Further gains could ensue after that. In the long term, classic growth stocks can provide the best returns over a full market cycle. Remember, most investors over-diversify; it's best to concentrate on your best ideas.

BORN Chicago, USA 1942.

EDUCATION Driehaus earned his B.Sc. in 1965 and in 1970 took an MBA at DePaul University's College of Commerce (now the Driehaus College of Business).

CAREER After 14 years as a stock analyst and fund manager, in 1979 Driehaus founded the brokerage Driehaus Securities Corporation LLC. Three years later he founded Driehaus Capital Management LLC, where he is still responsible for investments and chairs the board.

INVESTMENT PHILOSOPHY Driehaus is best categorized as an international growth investor. His cornerstones are accelerating sales and earnings plus relative price momentum. In addition, he looks for companies with strong, consistent, and sustained earnings growth. He is principally a bottom-up investor. He believes the application of technical analysis is essential to identify timely investments in attractive stocks and industries.

OTHER In 2000, Driehaus was named in Barron's 'All-Century' team as one of the 25 most influential people in the mutual-fund industry in the past hundred years. Driehaus has roughly $7.5 billion in assets under management. Through philanthropic- and community-service-oriented projects he supports conservation of classic architecture and the arts, reflecting his belief that beauty and the arts provide much-needed balance in a person's life.

Sources: Richard H. Driehaus; Driehaus Capital Management LLC; Mid Cap Growth Composite.

WILLIAM
DUNN
USA

ANNUAL YIELD
18%
for **37** YEARS
BENCHMARK 7%

→ Risk management is critical to survival.

→ Trading without an exit strategy invites disaster.

→ Anyone who tells you he can predict the future has probably not tested his predictions enough.

BORN Alton, Illinois, USA 1934.

EDUCATION Dunn earned a B.Sc. in Engineering Physics from the University of Kansas and a Ph.D. in Theoretical Physics from Northwestern University in 1966.

CAREER His studies complete, he conducted operation research for a variety of branches of the US military. Three years later he founded DUNN Capital Management in 1974. He recently left the day-to-day responsibility but still serves as chairman.

INVESTMENT PHILOSOPHY Dunn is a technical analyst and a pioneer of so-called quantitative trading, in which he has one of the longest and best track records. He relies 100 % on a systematic model used for a diversified futures trading portfolio. There are no emotions or fundamental analyses involved in the decision-making at all. The bulk of investments are commodities, but roughly half of the positions are based on currencies, stock markets, and interest rates. He and his team trade in over 50 futures market across the world.

OTHER Dunn created a computer program like many other traders to help with long-term commodity trading back in the days when computer programs were accessed via hundreds of IBM punch cards. One of the best profit contributions over the years has been the Japanese yen. Dunn's hobbies are skiing and travelling as well as playing with his grandchildren.

Sources: William Dunn; DUNN Capital.

ISRAEL A.
ENGLANDER
USA

ANNUAL YIELD
15%
for **21** YEARS
BENCHMARK 10%

E very successful manager has some kind of edge. That is how you get to be a successful manager. It is important to remain completely focused on taking advantage of that edge, and maintaining discipline.

Work on keeping the grass green on our side of the fence, and don't forget about looking over the fence at someone else's grass. The grass may look pretty green on the other side of the fence, but the fertilizer can be very expensive.

The days of being on top of trading, and leaving the risk management guys in a different room – if those days ever made sense, they are over now.

BORN Brooklyn, USA 1949.

EDUCATION Englander graduated from New York University with a degree in finance in 1970. He later started in the MBA programme there but dropped out shortly before finishing.

CAREER Englander began his career back office before landing a position as a floor trader on Amex. Convertibles, options, and merger arbitrage were his life until 1977, when he established a floor brokerage on the Amex that handled accounts for many of Wall Street's largest proprietary trading desks. Englander left the Amex floor in 1986 to establish an investment manager specializing in merger arbitrage. The company ceased trading in 1988 after its co-founder ran into legal problems. At the age of 40 he founded Millennium Management. He no longer trades himself, and focuses on managing the business.

INVESTMENT PHILOSOPHY Englander is a trader and hedge fund manager. Millennium Management is a multi-strategy fund that allocates capital to a variety of investment teams who work on their own strategies including: relative value; fundamental equity; statistical arbitrage/quantitative strategies; fixed income; and merger arbitrage/event-driven positions. Millennium is really a group of many different funds, but stock holdings account for the majority of the capital. All trading in the portfolios is concentrated on discovering misevaluations within and between various markets and instruments. The placement horizon is measured in hours. Grand placements are rare. Instead, there is a high degree of diversity, with many small gains. On a normal day, Millennium concludes between 1.5 and 2 million trades. 'I'm looking for instant gratification,' he says of his investing style. His investment thesis has three main components: a commitment to non-directional strategies, rigorous risk controls, and the discipline to adhere to these principles.

To fit in at Millennium, Englander says a trader's mindset has to be 'simpatico' with his own. To his mind there are no excuses for losing money: if a trader loses a certain amount, he is fired on the spot, or as he says, 'If you think you are so unlucky that after you sell, the market goes back up, then find another business. Go pray.'

OTHER Millennium manages roughly $15 billion, making it one of the biggest hedge funds worldwide. Since launch the fund has only had one negative year. It is now represented in many countries, with seventy employees in Asia, for example.

Englander's family was deported from Poland to a Soviet labour camp during the Second World War, and emigrated to the US in 1947. Englander started to trade stocks in high school. In 2012, Forbes estimated his wealth to be $2.3 billion.

Sources: Israel Englander – Absolute Return Symposium 2009; Millenium Management; Forbes; alchemyoffinanciers.com.

JEAN-MARIE EVEILLARD
USA

ANNUAL YIELD
14%
for **32** YEARS
BENCHMARK 9%

Value investing makes sense and it works – over time. Benjamin Graham's book *The Intelligent Investor* and Warren Buffett's letters to shareholders in Berkshire Hathaway's annual report are not about complex mathematical models; they're about common sense.

In 1984, Buffett showed that the returns – over time – of the value investors were much above average. In a 2004 update, the late Lou Lowenstein showed again that the returns over time of ten value funds (including our own First Eagle Global) were much above average. So why so few value investors? They're patient, long-term investors who therefore every now and then lag behind their peers and the benchmark. And to lag is to suffer. Value investors understand that the rewards come over time. No immediate gratification.

In the recent (and continuing) financial crisis, many value investors learned a lesson: it's no longer enough to be entirely bottom-up investors. A key question today is whether we are still in the economic and financial landscape of the post-Second World War period or are we in a new, so-far undefined landscape?

BORN Poitiers, France, 1940.

EDUCATION Eveillard is a graduate of Écoles des Hautes Études Commerciales, an esteemed French graduate school for business studies.

CAREER He started his career in 1962 with the French bank Société Générale until relocating to the US in 1968. Two years later, Eveillard began as an analyst with the SoGen International Fund. In 1979, he was appointed as the portfolio manager of the fund, later renamed the First Eagle Global Fund. After managing it for over thirty years, he now serves as senior adviser.

INVESTMENT PHILOSOPHY Eveillard is a long-term international stock market value investor, with a history of investing against the herd. In contrast to most value investors, he also has a top-down scenario. Another difference is in valuations, where he focuses on the enterprise value to EBIT. Preservation of capital is of highest priority. In general he buys stocks of companies that are financially safe, where there is very little or no debt, and whose intrinsic value is seen as being well above the current stock price. He is suspicious of low tax, which he thinks is usually a sign that profits are overstated. His remark 'I know the argument that you should only own your best 30 or 40 ideas, but I've never proven over time that I actually know in advance what those are' explains why he usually has more than 100 positions in his portfolios. He has kept a gold position in his funds as 'calamity insurance' for several years. He regards his investment style to be sometimes in the Benjamin Graham (deep-value) mode, but more often in the Warren Buffett mode.

OTHER Eveillard took the First Eagle Global Fund from $15 million to its current $20 billion in assets. He managed the fund alone for the first seven years. When Eveillard's successor abruptly resigned, he made a comeback aged 67. He is fond of the Austrian School of economics. In 2003, together with Ralph Wanger, he was the first to receive the Lifetime Achievement Award from Morningstar for building one of the most successful long-term records in the investment business. Through the Eveillard Family Charitable Trust he has provided support to a wide range of institutions in the arts, education, and social services. He enjoys going to the opera, and collects drawings in the same contrarian manner as he acquires securities.

Sources: Jean-Marie Eveillard; First Eagle Global Fund 1979–2011; Forbes, September 2009; Wikipedia.

MARC
FABER
SWITZERLAND/CHINA

THE SWISS ORACLE IN CHINA

Be very careful of any forecast. Usually, analysts, fund managers, and strategists can foresee the future only when it coincides with their own wishes, whereas they ignore the most obvious facts when these facts are not welcome.

Watch day and night (the latter very important) with curiosity what is happening around you because the greatest investment opportunities are always hidden in the most unlikely places.

We all need to remind ourselves that we have no idea how the world will look like in five years, let alone ten. Therefore, some of our business or investment decisions will be very wrong. But, what we need to focus upon is what the consequences could be, if we are wrong.

Investors mostly fail because they find it very hard to do nothing. But by spending a day in a round of strenuous idleness without your mobile phone and Blackberry, you may see the future more clearly. Remember, patience is also a form of action.

BORN Zurich, Switzerland 1946.

EDUCATION Faber studied economics at the University of Zurich and, at the age of 24, obtained a Ph.D. in Economics.

CAREER Between 1970 and 1978, Faber worked for the investment bank White Weld & Company Ltd. in New York, Zurich, and Hong Kong. Since 1973, he has lived in Hong Kong. From 1978 to February 1990, he was the managing director of Drexel Burnham Lambert (HK) Ltd. In June 1990, he set up his own business, Marc Faber Ltd., which acts as an investment advisor and fund manager. In addition, he publishes a widely read monthly investment newsletter The Gloom Boom & Doom Report, writes books, and is a regular contributor to several leading financial publications around the world.

INVESTMENT PHILOSOPHY Faber invests and advises all over the world in almost all asset classes. He relies on his command of economic history as well as his time as a trader. He focuses on macro, strategy and gold. For people in the investment community, he is maybe known as the most notorious bear in the market and at the same time a contrarian investor. The first is not always true. He has made several bullish calls, of which Brazil stocks in 1990s and world stock market in spring 2009 are the most remembered. The following cornerstones advice gives a sense of his investment philosophy: (i) Everything comes to the investor who buys out-of-favour and neglected assets. (ii) The best way to make money is to buy value stocks: low price to sales, low price to book, low price to cash flow, high dividend yield. (iii) Never forget to diversify properly. (iv) Never get carried away by a lucky investment with outsized gains. (v) Stay single!

Even if he digs into specific stocks and sectors he spends most time on the macro level. He is keen on the Austrian School of economics.

OTHER He is well-known for being prescient about the 2008 financial crisis; the Asian crisis months before it happened; warning his clients to cash out before Black Monday in 1987; forecasting the burst in the Japanese bubble in 1990; correctly predicting the collapse in US gaming stocks in 1993; foreseeing the Asia-Pacific financial crisis of 1997/98; and so on. His mantra is 'Follow the course opposite to custom and you will almost always be right'. His book *Tomorrow's Gold* was for several weeks on Amazon's best-seller list. The Gloom Boom & Doom Report uses economic, social, and historical trends to warn investors when investment themes have become widely accepted and are, therefore, highly priced and risky, while it continuously searches for opportunities in unloved and depressed markets. His web site is illustrated with 17th century paintings of "The Dance of Death" and he is nicknamed Dr Doom. He has a collection of a quarter of a million Mao badges and has a ponytail.

Sources: Marc Faber; gloomboomdoom.com; Wikipedia.

MICHAEL
FARMER
UK

ANNUAL YIELD
15%
for 8 YEARS

BENCHMARK 3%

→ Go where there is little risk, but where there is potential for great reward—Opportunity
→ Don't get euphoric!—Wife's wisdom
→ Sell what you haven't got and buy what you don't want—Contrarian
→ Fear God, not man—We're not here forever

BORN Kent, UK 1944.

EDUCATION Secondary school.

CAREER Farmer left school at 18 and went to work at A. J. Strauss, a metals trading firm in the City. He started as a 'difference account clerk'. Between 1984 and 1989, he managed the non-ferrous metals positions at Philipp Brothers, the biggest global metal trader of that period. He left in 1989 to form the Metal & Commodity Company, a subsidiary of Metallgesellschaft AG, which became the world's largest trader in physical copper and nickel and was floated on the London stock market in 1999. One year later it was sold to Enron. After taking two years off to study the Bible he founded RK Capital Management with two partners in 2004.

INVESTMENT PHILOSOPHY Farmer is a commodity investor specializing in copper. His road to success is concentration, experience, and profound knowledge. He and his team try to be more up-to-date about the copper market – both suppliers and customers – than anyone else. Often being contrarian in this highly volatile market also requires a big portion of guts and stamina. In 2006 the fund was up by 188 % followed by 50 % decline the year after. Farmer probably stands for one of the most volatile investments in this book. This, despite the fact that he does not deal much in options and futures, but instead trades physical base metals between producers and consumers. Farmer says his faith makes him a better money manager by keeping him humble.

OTHER He is nicknamed Mr. Copper and he is regarded as one of the most successful commodity traders in the world. He and his team manage at present £1.3 billion. In 2011 he topped Bloomberg's league of global mid-cap hedge-fund returns, and was named the most successful small hedge-fund manager in the world. Farmer is often responsible for shipping around 15–20 % of China's copper supplies. He has donated £2.3 million to the British Tories and in 2012 was appointed co-treasurer of the Conservative Party. He is an active Christian.

Sources: Michael Farmer; RK Capital Management; Bloomberg; Wikipedia.

KEN
FISHER
USA

ANNUAL YIELD
9.3%
for **16** YEARS
....
BENCHMARK 4.9%

Always know you could be wrong and will be a lot. There are two subsets here. Many focus on how smart they are compared to others, and presume if they're smarter that is sufficient. Wrong! Capital markets move on the unexpected, and being a smarter processor of the same information everyone else bases decisions on doesn't get you that far or provide that much extra value. Capital markets theory is clear: you have to somehow, some way, know something others don't know. That's very hard to do, and even when you think you do, you're often wrong. Second, by measurement, even the most legendary investors end up being wrong a lot in the long term. Most investors are more wrong than right. A small percentage is right more than wrong in the long term. Everyone is wrong a lot, and if you can be right 70 per cent of the time in the long term you end up a living legend, which means by the same token you'll be wrong fully 30 per cent of the time, and often for long enough time periods it feels like forever; so get used to being wrong.

Whatever you did today won't work ten years from now—so you always have to be thinking down the road about the next new thing that might work. Everything changes. Things I did successfully decades ago I wouldn't attempt at all now. Thirty-five years ago I could find things in obscure trade journals in musty libraries and similar off-the-wall sources that might not have been discounted into market pricing. But today all that would be subject to an Internet search and known widely, and priced easily, so a different tack is needed. Once I could make money simply buying low price-to-sales ratio stocks. Not so now, unless it is a timing thing tied to when value is super hot. The time between when something seems new and seems to work in the markets and when it is overly popular and priced to oblivion seems ever faster as time rolls on, and that is likely to continue. The lesson I've learned is that pace continues, and will carry on doing so. Don't lose your sense of who you are—you want to hang on to that—but expect all tactics to become rapidly obsolete.

The prime lesson of behaviouralism in the last thirty years is not how stupid everyone is or some behavioural trick you can apply to outmanoeuvre others in the marketplace, but that behaviouralism itself is about knowing yourself—and the most important lesson to learn from it is where you're prone to blindside yourself, which everyone does; where you're prone to over-confidence, which everyone is; and where you have natural cognitive errors. Perhaps the best question to ask yourself is, 'What am I doing to blindside myself right now?' Parallel to this is 'What do I believe that's false?' But often the answer to that second question derives from a cognitive error in our brains that could be corrected by knowing yourself better and better knowing your behavioural shortcomings.

BORN San Francisco, USA 1950.

EDUCATION Fisher graduated in Economics from Humboldt State University in 1972, after first studying forestry.

CAREER After graduating, Fisher worked for his father, Philip Fisher, who was a noted money manager and author. Fisher started his own company, Fisher Investments, aged 29, in 1979. He still serves as chairman and CEO.

INVESTMENT PHILOSOPHY Fisher is best described as an evolutionary investor, changing and using what he regards as the best investment approach for the moment. In the Seventies he pioneered and successfully worked with the price-to-sales ratio (PSR) method. For the time being, he is more focused on capitalizing on themes and sector cycles as they come into and out of favour. In general, Fisher is a top-down investor, with a political and global perspective to his analyses. When it comes to stocks, which is his home turf, he bases his selection on screening. No visits to companies for him!

OTHER Fisher's firm manages over $40 billion and is considered one of the largest independent discretionary money managers in the US. He may be best known for his 27-year tenure as Forbes's portfolio strategy columnist – the fourth longest-running columnist in Forbes 90-plus-year history. In 11 of the 16 last years he has beaten the market in terms of stock picks in Forbes. On average, his Forbes picks have outperformed the S&P 500 by 4.4 % annually. Fisher has received many awards and been listed as one of the industry's 30 most influential people over the last 30 years by Investment Advisor. He has written eight books, most of them national bestsellers. In addition to PSR, he has spearheaded other analytical tools, such as the price-to-research ratio (PRR), and conducted academic research on consumer behaviour. Fisher was ranked 263 on the 2011 Forbes 400 list of richest Americans. He has located, excavated, and catalogued more than thirty-five pre-1920 steam-era redwood lumber mills.

Sources: Ken Fisher: Fisher Investments; Forbes; Wikipedia.

PHILIP
FISHER
USA

THE FATHER OF QUALITATIVE ANALYSIS

Ten don'ts for investors:

→ Don't buy into promotional companies.

→ Don't ignore a good stock just because it trades 'over the counter'.

→ Don't buy a stock just because you like the 'tone' of its annual report.

→ Don't assume that the high price at which a stock may be selling in relation to earnings is necessarily an indication that further growth in those earnings has largely been already discounted in the price.

→ Don't quibble over eights and quarters.

→ Don't overstress diversification

→ Don't be afraid to buy on a war scare.

→ Don't forget your Gilbert and Sullivan – don't be influenced by what doesn't matter.

→ Don't fail to consider time as well as price in buying a true growth stock.

→ Don't follow the crowd.

BORN San Francisco, USA 1907. Died 2004.

EDUCATION Fisher studied business at Stanford University.

CAREER Fisher's career began in 1928 when he dropped out of the newly created Stanford Business School to work as a securities analyst with the Anglo-London Bank in San Francisco. Soon he switched to a stock exchange firm for a short time before he had to leave. He started his own money management business Fisher & Company in 1931, and he managed the company's affairs until his retirement in 1999 at the age of 91.

INVESTMENT PHILOSOPHY Fisher pioneered the growth investment strategy in the stock market. The investment was based on fundamentals, and it can be argued that he mixed value and growth. Although he began some fifty years before the name Silicon Valley became known, he specialized in innovative companies driven by research and development. He practised long-term investing, and strove to buy great companies at reasonable prices. Target investments should have higher profit margins and higher sales growth than the industry; be the technologically most advanced company in the sector; no dividend; a high return on capital; a commitment to research and development; superior sales organization; and proprietary products or services. Managements should have integrity, conservative accounting, accessibility and good long-term outlook, openness to change, excellent financial controls, and good staff policies. In terms of valuation, the ratio of the current price-earnings ratio to the estimated growth rate in earnings per share (PEG ratio) should be greater than 0.1 and less than or equal to 0.5. High P/E ratio was not a problem. He avoided investing in old, famous companies.

Deep research was, according to Fisher, the key to successful investing. He was said to be superb at networking, and searched far and wide for information on a company, a process he called 'scuttlebutt'. His quote 'I don't want a lot of good investments; I want a few outstanding ones' speaks volumes about his views on diversifying, and he said that the best time to sell a good stock was 'almost never'. He held onto both Texas Instruments and Motorola for almost 50 years.

OTHER There are no official figures for his performance, but his few clients – he refused to take on more than thirty and never managed more than $500 million – witness to extraordinary performance. Motorola appreciated more than twentyfold versus a sevenfold appreciation of the S&P 500 during his time as a shareholder. He influenced both the value investors and the way to work. Perhaps the best known of Fisher's followers is Warren Buffett, who has said on some occasions that 'he is 85 % Graham and 15 % Fisher'. It was said he never worked at the weekend, and finished at 4 o'clock every day. He wrote four books of which *Common Stocks and Uncommon Profits*, a guide to investing, has remained in print ever since it was first published in 1958.

....

Sources: Philip Fisher, *Common Stocks and Uncommon Profits* (1958); Forbes; Wikipedia.

ALBERT FRÈRE
BELGIUM

THE MASTER OF TIMING

→ Perform only those investments that you understand.

→ I suffer from insomnia when I am in debt.

→ Amat victoria curam – Victory favours those who take pains.

→ In every danger, an opportunity.

BORN Charleroi, Belgium 1926.

EDUCATION Dropped out of secondary school.

CAREER Aged 17, after his father died, he took over the running of the family's nail merchant business. Aged 30 he began investing in steel factories which, when he sold them in late 1970s, became the foundation for his wealth. He continued to buy and sell, mainly Belgian national companies, and has today an empire of media, oil, and utilities.

INVESTMENT PHILOSOPHY Frère has displayed impeccable timing in his dealings. His strength and strategy predicting changes is business structure, political impact, and long evolutionary trends in industries. He was, for example, the pioneer in Europe on cross-border deals. He foresaw the single European market and the consolidation that would be one consequence of the EU. The valuation is not always the crucial point for him in making decisions, and he invests in both public and private companies. This investment strategy demands specific skills and contacts, and is not easy to apply.

OTHER Frère keeps himself well out of the limelight. He rarely gives interviews (I thank him for granting me one!) or speaks in public. According to Forbes his wealth is an estimated $3.6 billion in 2012, which makes him the richest individual in Belgium. At the age of 85 he made one of his biggest deals so far taking the investment conglomerate CNP private. He is a hunter, athlete, and lover of fine wine. Frère took up golf in his seventies.

Sources: Albert Frère; Wikipedia; Forbes.

MARIO
GABELLI
USA

ANNUAL YIELD
16.3%
for **33** YEARS
BENCHMARK 11.3%

Buy what you know. Develop a core competency in an industry or industries and invest there. Become an expert – read every trade publication, talk to every company management (public or private), and go to every company and industry presentation in your area of competence. Do hard work. Create spreadsheets on companies you want to buy, breaking out earnings, cash flows, and private market values for each stock. Model the numbers for the next five years. Focus on companies that have a stock price below intrinsic value. Look for a margin of safety. Look for a catalyst or event that will help surface values. Then remember investing is for the long term.

Work hard – that's the best advice I can give anyone. The world is full of smart people. Those who are smart and are also willing to make sacrifices to truly excel in their profession will be the biggest successes.

I think the real bargains are what they would call the smaller, ignored, and unloved companies.

BORN New York, USA 1942.

EDUCATION Gabelli graduated from Fordham University summa cum laude (now renamed the Gabelli School of Business Administration after a $25 million donation) and took an MBA at Columbia Business School in 1967.

CAREER After graduation, Gabelli started as an analyst at Loeb, Rhoades & Co. In 1977, aged 35, Gabelli formed Gabelli & Company, Inc., a brokerage house (later GAMCO Investors, Inc.). In February 1999, the company went public. He still serves as chairman and CEO for the company as well as chief investment officer and portfolio manager.

INVESTMENT PHILOSOPHY Gabelli is a bottom-up stock value investor and a disciple of Graham and Dodd's valuation theory. However, he carved out his own valuation niche by analysing a firm in great detail to calculate its private-market value (PMV). GAMCO looks for securities in companies that appear underpriced relative to the PMV with catalysts to unlock the value. The PMV–which is now a trademark and widely used by private equity companies – is the price a strategic buyer is willing to pay for the entire company. In addition, Gabelli is more focused on free cash flow than earnings, even if the earnings trend is an important cornerstone. He is famous for his endurance – he can wait for years for an investment to bear fruit. It is more often than not a contrarian investment approach. He describes his investment philosophy with the equation 'Graham & Dodd + Buffett = Gabelli'.

OTHER GAMCO manages over $30 billion in assets, and Gabelli has won several awards, of which inclusion in Barron's All-Century Team is one of the more notable. Additionally, Gabelli was named the domestic equity Fund Manager of the Year in 1997 by Morningstar and Money Manager of the Year by Institutional Investor in 2010. Gabelli bought his first stock when he was thirteen years old and recommends reading annual reports instead of novels. He is also a philanthropist with a particular interest in education. Gabelli is a frequent commentator on television and in the newspapers as well as maintaining a strong public Twitter presence.

Sources: Mario Gabelli; Gabelli Asset Fund; GAMCO Investor; Wikipedia.

FRANCISCO
GARCÍA PARAMÉS
SPAIN

ANNUAL YIELD
17.5%
for **18** YEARS

BENCHMARK 9.5%

Personality vs intelligence: 90 % of investors with whom we discuss our investments agree on the attractive nature of these investments. But only a very small proportion are prepared to take the next steps: invest and then wait for as long as necessary. One must be able to ignore market movements and any institutional obligations, even emphasize one's convictions by increasing the investment when the markets do not look favourable. In short, it is essential to know oneself, and along with a normal IQ, the determining factor will be character.

A good backup to these qualities is references. For anyone (particularly in Madrid, which is not renowned for its investing tradition), the sense of security achieved by following in the steps of an experienced investor is very important. Both in the good times (when in either absolute or relative terms, things are going well) and the bad, analysing the careers of investors who have been through similar situations allows one to act with conviction and maintain a long term view, something which can sometimes be lost.

Never stop learning: When we invest, we must have strong conviction and determi-

nation in the process. To have permanent doubts is pointless, in spite of the fact that uncertainty is a constant. But that conviction must go hand in hand with a permanent capacity to learn – not an easy thing to do. For example, a couple of years ago at Bestinver, following a good track record over the previous fifteen years, we came across a (little) book by a well-known investor which caused us to fine-tune our strategies, although without actually altering the essentials. It is not easy to conjugate 'conviction' and 'open mind' in the same sentence, but it must be done!

Economic framework: The majority of well-known investors command a relatively superficial knowledge of the so-called 'economy'. I arrived at the Austrian School of economics after eight years as an investor, and I did so precisely because it provided a theoretical framework to what I was seeing every day in the market, namely, human action. Only here it was it explained in incentives, objectives, consequences, etc – that is, life itself. Thanks to Mises and Hayek, among others, we can navigate through an investors' world with a compass that shows us over which waters we can sail, and which we cannot.

BORN Galicia, Spain 1963.

EDUCATION García Paramés has an Economics degree from the Complutense University of Madrid, and took an MBA at the IESE Business School (Barcelona) 1989.

CAREER García Paramés started his career at Bestinver as a stock analyst in 1989. His passion for investment led him to asset management, and he was soon named CIO of the company, where he remains to this day.

INVESTMENT PHILOSOPHY García Paramés's management style is based on the strict application of the principles of value investment (Graham, Buffett, etc.), within a framework of a profound knowledge of the Austrian School's theory of economic cycles. Pricing power and cash flow are important parameters in the analyses. García Paramés avoids investments where he cannot forecast the next ten years. During the last few years the portfolio has shifted to only include quality companies. He never fights the management.

OTHER Nicknamed 'the Warren Buffett of Europe', his more recent fund, Bestinver Internacional (Global Equity Fund), launched 1998, has an annual return of almost 11 %, beating the benchmark (1 %) by a factor of more than ten. He is a self-taught investor, similar to some of the other superstars. It is especially impressive since he is from Spain, which has no long tradition of investing. He speaks and reads five languages.

....

Sources: Francisco García Paramés; Bestinver; Wikipedia.

BENJAMIN GRAHAM
USA

ANNUAL YIELD
20%
for **30** YEARS
BENCHMARK 4.5%

→ Know what you are doing – know your business.

→ Do not let anyone else run your business, unless (i) you can supervise his performance with adequate care and comprehension, or (ii) you have unusually strong reasons for placing implicit confidence in his integrity and ability.

→ Do not enter upon an operation – that is, manufacturing or trading in an item –unless a reliable calculation shows that it has a fair chance to yield a reasonable profit. In particular, keep away from ventures in which you have little to gain and much to lose.

→ Have the courage of your knowledge and experience. If you have formed a conclusion from the facts, and if you know your judgement is sound, act on it – even though others may hesitate or differ.

BORN London, UK 1894. Died 1976.

EDUCATION He graduated in Economics from Columbia University in 1914.

CAREER After university he immediately went to work for a Wall Street firm, Newburger, Henderson & Loeb. By 1920, he was a partner in the firm. Aged 30 Graham formed an investment partnership with Jerome Newman (Graham-Newman). Two years later he also started teaching advanced security analysis at Columbia University, and continued to do so until his retirement in 1956. The same year saw the end of the Graham-Newman partnership.

INVESTMENT PHILOSOPHY Graham is the intellectual father of value investing and founded the value school. He observed that paying less than intrinsic value is 'value investing', and the larger the gap between 'price' and 'value', the higher the margin of safety – safety from the perspective of losing money. Graham wanted to buy stocks selling at two-thirds or less of their intrinsic value. Graham's philosophy was, first and foremost, to preserve capital, and then to try to make it grow. He suggested having 25 % to 75 % of your investments in bonds, and varying this based on market conditions. He also introduced the mindset that you invest in a business, and the value is not dependent on the next quarterly earnings, but what price you would be willing to pay for the entire business today.

Grahams approach was mostly quantitative, fairly static, mathematical, and mainly focused on the balance sheet and history. He did not talk to company management. His investment characteristics tend to be strong balance sheets, above-average profit margins, and ample cash flow. The investments also needed to have uninterrupted dividends for 20 years and increased earnings per share by at least 30 % over the previous 10 years. It was no buy-and-hold strategy, and he recommended that investors sell when the stock went up more than 50 % or after two years. The disadvantage of the strategy, as he preached it, was that it was such a good method that practically everybody knew it and picked up on the things that met his formula, so that by the mid-1970s his view was that the investment community had adopted his strategy in a way that he doubted whether such an extensive effort could generate sufficiently superior selections to justify the costs. He then decided to modify his investment strategy.

OTHER After losing almost everything in the 1929 crash and the Great Depression, he devised a risk-averse approach to playing the market, one that distinguished between investment and speculation. Graham did not lose money any single year after that, despite two world wars and the 50 % stock market crash in 1973–74. He created a new template for how to approach the market, thinking about volatility as being in your favour instead of being a threat. The phrase Mr. Market – which he argued should be treated as a manic-depressive – was coined by Graham. He wrote several books, of which *The Intelligent Investor* (1949) is according to Warren Buffett 'the best book about investing ever written'. He was a born lecturer and taught a dozen other investors in this book. Outside Wall Street his interests included Greek and Latin classics and languages in general – he translated several books from Portuguese.

Sources: Benjamin Graham, *Security Analyses* (1934), and *The Intelligent Investor.* (1949); Graham-Newman, Forbes; Wikipedia.

JEREMY
GRANTHAM
UK

ANNUAL YIELD
10%
for **24** YEARS
BENCHMARK 8%

Believe in history. In investing, Santayana is right: history repeats and repeats itself, forget it at your peril. All bubbles break, all investment frenzies pass away. You absolutely must ignore the vested interests of the industry and the inevitable cheerleaders who will assure you that this time it's a new high plateau or a permanently higher level of productivity, even if that view comes from the Federal Reserve itself. No. Make that, especially if it comes from there. The market is gloriously inefficient and wanders far from fair price, but eventually, after breaking your heart and your patience (and, for professionals, those of their clients too), it will go back to fair value. Your task is to survive until that happens.

'Neither a lender nor a borrower be'. If you borrow to invest, it will interfere with your survivability. Unleveraged portfolios cannot be stopped out; leveraged portfolios can. Leverage reduces the investor's critical asset: patience. (To digress, excessive borrowing has turned out to be an even bigger curse than Polonius could have known. It encourages finan-

cial aggressiveness, recklessness, and greed. It increases your returns over and over until, suddenly, it ruins you. For individuals, it allows you to have today what you really can't afford until tomorrow. It has proven to be so seductive that individuals en masse have shown themselves incapable of resisting it, as if it were a drug. Governments also, from the Middle Ages onwards and especially now, it seems, have proven themselves equally incapable of resistance. Any sane society must recognize the lure of debt and pass laws accordingly. Interest payments must absolutely not be tax deductible or preferred in any way. Governments must apparently be treated like Polonius' children and given limits. By law, cumulative government debt should be given a sensible limit of, say, 50 per cent of GDP, with current transgressions given ten or twenty years to be corrected.) Don't put all your treasure in one boat. This is about as obvious as any investment advice could be. It was a literal truth learned by merchants thousands of years ago. Several different investments, the more the merrier, will give your portfolio resilience, the ability to withstand shocks. Clearly, the more investments you have and the more different they are, the more likely you are to survive those critical periods when your big bets move against you.

Be patient and focus on the long term. Wait for the good cards. If you've waited and waited some more until finally a very cheap market appears, this will be your margin of safety. Now all you have to do is withstand the pain as the very good investment becomes exceptional. Individual stocks usually recover, entire markets always do. If you've followed the previous rules, you will outlast the bad news.

Recognize your advantages over the professionals. By far the biggest problem for professionals in investing is dealing with career and business risk: protecting your own job as an agent. The second curse of professional investing is over-management caused by the need to be seen to be busy, to be earning your keep. The individual is far better positioned to wait patiently for the right pitch while paying no regard to what others are doing, which is almost impossible for professionals.

BORN Doncaster, UK 1944.

EDUCATION Grantham studied Economics at the University of Sheffield, and in 1966 completed an MBA at Harvard University.

CAREER He began his investment career as an economist with Royal Dutch Shell. In 1969 he was co-founder of Batterymarch Financial Management. Seven years later, aged 33, Grantham co-founded GMO where he is chief investment strategist and is an active member of GMO's asset allocation division and member of the board.

INVESTMENT PHILOSOPHY Grantham is an asset allocator and his philosophy can be summarized by his commonly used phrase 'reversion to the mean'. Essentially, he believes that all asset classes and markets will revert to mean historical levels from highs and lows. His firm seeks to understand historical changes in markets and predict results for seven years into the future.

OTHER Grantham has built much of his investing reputation by correctly identifying speculative market 'bubbles' as they were happening. Grantham avoided investing in Japanese equities, real estate in the late eighties, the dot-com bubble as well as financial stocks 2008. He is founder of the Grantham Foundation with the mission to protect and improve the health of the global environment.

Sources: Jeremy Grantham GMO quarterly letter February 2012; Global Asset Allocation; Wikipedia.

GLENN H. GREENBERG
USA

ANNUAL YIELD
17.8%
for **26** YEARS

BENCHMARK 10.4%

K now your sphere of competence and stay within its bounds. It is tempting – mostly from inflated ego – to think that success in one endeavour means one will be equally adept in some other. Bad idea. This may also happen when there is not much to do in one's usual hunting grounds. My own experience has been to lose money when I have strayed.

Beware of the false precision implied in financial modelling. The future is just as unknowable when projected out on a spreadsheet to many decimal points as it is when written on the back of an envelope. The difference is that the person using the paper scrap knows he is making a rough estimate and therefore must leave plenty of room for miscalculation; not so the PC modeller, who incorporates every historical number into his complex analysis and thereby derives a false sense of certainty about his future projections.

Ask yourself often the following question: given everything I know, how much of my net worth do I want to have in each stock in my portfolio? This is not meant to encourage a lot of trading, but should occasionally push you to buy more of something that is down from where it was purchased, and lighten or eliminate a stock that has done extremely well but no longer offers an adequate return.

Keep things simple. Complexity generally involves added risk, whether you know it or not.

BORN New York, USA 1947.

EDUCATION He graduated from Phillips Academy and Yale and took a Master's degree in English at New York University, while teaching for three years and waiting out the Vietnam War. In 1973 he took an MBA from Columbia Business School.

CAREER Greenberg started as an analyst at Morgan Guaranty Trust, and was soon promoted to portfolio manager. Five years later he joined Central National–Gottesman Corporation, working as an analyst for the legendary investor Arthur Ross. Aged 37 Greenberg founded Chieftain Capital together with John Shapiro to manage money for wealthy individuals. After 23 years, Chieftain Capital reached over $5 billion in assets under management. In 2009, aged 62, the partners of Chieftain Capital split up, and Greenberg went on to found Brave Warrior Advisors.

INVESTMENT PHILOSOPHY Greenberg is a bottom-up stock market investor. He is regarded as a value investor, but has a slightly different approach due to his focus on industry market structure. Very few value investors would have invested, as Greenberg did, in Google. He looks for companies that have zero or very few competitors and a deep moat. The growth should be gradual rather than steep. He likes a predictive view of where he thinks the business can be in a few years' time. The starting-point is the free cash flow yield today and how much he thinks the business is capable of growing over the next few years. He also places a great deal of emphasis on return on invested capital. The method results in a portfolio of high-quality businesses where he has high confidence in the fundamentals and can hold the stocks through severe markets. He runs a concentrated portfolio with usually no more than a dozen names. He believes that the more companies you own, the less you will know about each, and the less you know about a business, the more likely you are to make mistakes due to fear and greed. He disregards sell-side reports and holds the stocks on average five years. He is sometimes vocal about investments to put pressure on management.

OTHER At present he manages above $1 billion. Greenberg enjoys guest lecturing at Columbia's Business School. He has been ranked fourth in the nation in squash, plays the guitar, and has seven children.

Sources: Glenn H. Greenberg; Chieftain Capital; Brave Warrior; Wikipedia.

NIWES
HEMVACHIRAVARAKORN
THAILAND

ANNUAL YIELD
38.4%
for **15** YEARS
BENCHMARK 1.8%

Embrace a crisis. Turn it into an opportunity. Sometimes, bad news is good news. Stockmarket crises often offer great opportunities for long-term investors to buy great companies' stocks at amazingly cheap prices otherwise impossible in normal market conditions. Case in point: during the great crash in 2008, the Thai stockmarket dropped 50 % along with the world market. Being fully invested at that time, I decided to borrow to invest more. This turned out to be an excellent move, because by the next year, the market returned at a stacker rate of over 60 %, providing my portfolio a return of over 140 %.

Find a great company going through trouble. Solvable trouble, that is. Because one of the greatest investments is the one involving an investment in a great firm while it is experiencing a trouble that can be fixed. When you find such company, do not hesitate to buy a big chunk of it. Its stock prices will eventually rise spectacularly when the problem is solved (which often doesn't take very long).

Stick to a winning strategy. The best strategy for long-term investment is to invest in companies that have consistently growing earnings for over long periods of time (at least 5–7 years). Holding a portfolio of such companies (at least 5–7 stocks) could almost guarantee an above-satisfactory return, no matter what condition the stockmarket is in. In the long run, your portfolio will beat the market strikingly.

BORN Bangkok, Thailand 1953.

EDUCATION Hemvachiravarakorn received his engineering degree from Chulalongkorn University in 1976. He took an MBA in marketing and received a Ph.D. in finance aged 32.

CAREER Hemvachiravarakorn has spent most of his career in the field of finance, in financial planning, investment banking, stock portfolio investment, and corporate lending. His last job was as vice-president of a bank. As of 2003, he has managed his own wealth full-time.

INVESTMENT PHILOSOPHY Hemvachiravarakorn is a value investor. The focus is purely on stocks. His most important parameters in investing are growing companies with competitive advantages in marketing; healthy financial status; and those with low capital investments. A cornerstone is to never invest in companies with return on equity below 15 %. To adopt value investing in Thailand he needed to be more flexible in the requirement of history for the target due to the young market.

OTHER Hemvachiravarakorn has written more than ten books on the subject of value investing and has been acclaimed as the 'Guru of Value Investment' or 'The Warren Buffett of Thailand'. He is also a columnist for a business newspaper.

Sources: Niwes Hemvachiravarakorn.

IAN
HENDERSON
UK

ANNUAL YIELD
16%
for **12** YEARS
BENCHMARK 8%

→ Don't invest in things you don't understand.
→ Be prepared to be patient. Sometimes the market can be slow to recognize change, and remember that long-term trends can go on for years.
→ An idea is only as good as the management implementing it.

BORN London, UK 1949.

EDUCATION Henderson graduated in Philosophy, Politics, and Law from Edinburgh University.

CAREER He began his career with five years as an accountant with Peat Marwick Mitchell & Co. Another five years was spent at Morgan Grenfell as an international portfolio manager followed by nine years as CIO at Wardley Investment Services Ltd. Since 1991 he has managed the JPMorgan flagship fund Natural Resources. He stepped down in January 2012, but remained in an advisory capacity until March 2013.

INVESTMENT PHILOSOPHY Henderson is an international commodity investor with a slight preference for value-based investment opportunities. His cornerstones in investing in the high volatile commodity business are: (i) Be conscious of the consensus. It's better to spot implausible assumptions such as using price assumptions that are completely at variance with spot and forward prices. (ii) Assumptions of mean reversion need to be scrutinized because the future does not replicate the past. (iii) It is extremely important to be aware of changes in fashion and trends, for example commodity substitution. (iv) Never be afraid to run winners, as trends within commodities tend to last longer than expected. (v) Never invest more than you can afford to lose. (vi) Only do things you believe in yourself, not because others believe them. (vii) Do not panic when markets crash; the world is unlikely to end.

OTHER All in all he was responsible for almost £10 billion in assets and widely considered the best commodities manager in the City. Horse racing and hunting are two of his preferred activities outside work.

Sources: Ian Henderson; JPM Natural Resources.

JOHN W. HENRY
USA

ANNUAL YIELD
20%
for **27** YEARS

It's important to have a plan, remain disciplined in executing that plan, and pay attention to what is actually happening rather than what you expect to happen. We try to be as objective as possible in our analyses. It's not always easy for people who are involved every day to stay with a plan when misfortune occurs for a time. You always encounter the unexpected, and this can push discipline right out of the way in the name of prudence. But prudence almost always dictates staying with the approach that has made you successful. I see that as one of my primary roles. I often encourage everyone during difficult days to remain patient. I don't blame people for the unexpected.

We can't always take advantage of a particular period. But in an uncertain world, perhaps the investment philosophy that makes the most sense, if you study the implications carefully, is trend following. Trend following consists of buying high and selling low. For nineteen years we have consistently bought high and sold low. If trends were not the underlying nature of markets, our type of trading would have very quickly put us out of business. It wouldn't take nineteen years, or even nineteen months, of buying high and selling low ALL the time to bankrupt you. But trends are an integral, underlying reality in life. How can someone buy high and sell low and be successful for two decades unless the underlying nature of markets is to trend? On the other hand, I've seen year after year brilliant men successfully buying low and selling high for a while, and then going broke because they thought they understood why a certain investment instrument had to perform in accordance with their personal logic. We stick to our knitting.

If you can put aside what should be, what could be, what ought to be, and what would have, could have, should have occurred and just pay attention to what is actually happening, the act of paying attention transforms what is. The greatest action, the wisest, the best action that you can take in almost any situation is to stay with what is, instead of jumping to conclusions or trying to come up with conclusions. Just pay attention. And that has had more of an impact on my trading and my life than any other thing.

BORN Quincy, Illinois, USA 1949.

EDUCATION Henry studied at the University of California where he majored in philosophy but did not graduate – partly the result of performing on the road in two rock bands, Elysian Fields and Hillary.

CAREER His father died when Henry was 25, and he took over his family's 2,000-acre farm. He then started to speculate in corn, wheat, and soybeans, and taught himself hedging techniques. He became a commodity-trading adviser. Eight years later, in 1982, he started John W. Henry & Company, Inc. (JWH), which is now one of the oldest established managed futures advisors in the world.

INVESTMENT PHILOSOPHY Henry is a commodity future trader who developed a mechanical trend-following method for the futures market. The system trading decisions are based on an explicit intention of precluding not only human emotion, but also any subjective evaluation of fundamentals. His mantra is that no one can predict the future. Another cornerstone is patience. Henry is convinced that long-term holdings are the best approach for performance over time, and he is said to be one of the most long-term traders in the futures market. JWH operates worldwide in the futures market and in categories such as commodities, metals, energy, currencies, interest rates, and stock indexes. Despite the diversification, JWH has huge volatility in historic performance.

OTHER Due to different investment programmes started and ended over the years I have estimated performance. The Financial and Metals programme had a compounded average return of 29 % between 1984 and the year 2000. The oldest programme at present (from 1997) runs at 12 % (benchmark 5 %) compounded annual return. The assets under management at JWH have plummeted more than 90 % over the past five years and are now below $300 million. According to Forbes, Henry's net worth is $1.1 billion. Henry is a big supporter and investor in various sports: he is the principal owner of the Boston Red Sox and Liverpool F.C. to name a few.

....

Sources: John W. Henry; Michael Covel, *Trend Following. Learn to Make Millions in Up or Down Markets* (2004); CME Magazine; Turtletrading.com; Wikipedia.

MICHAEL
HINTZE
UK

ANNUAL YIELD
21%
for **9** YEARS
BENCHMARK 1%

→ The market price of an equity is driven by three elements: fundamentals, technical, and sentiment. For either a long or short trade to work, all three need to be aligned.

→ In trading currencies, the key is not the macroeconomic numbers, but rather whether the central bank is providing a loose or tight monetary policy.

→ Fraud is the hardest 'risk' to hedge and potentially one that is extremely difficult to unearth. It is why one needs strong fundamental analysis and crosschecks.

BORN Harbin, China 1953

EDUCATION Hintze holds a B.Sc. in Physics and Pure Mathematics and a B.Eng. in Electrical Engineering both from the University of Sydney. He also holds an M.Sc. in Acoustics from the University of New South Wales and an MBA from Harvard Business School.

CAREER After serving for three years in the Australian Regular Army as a captain he began his career as an electrical design engineer for Civil and Civic Pty Ltd. in Australia. Moving to the US, he started to work for Salomon Brothers as a fixed income trader. In 1984 he moved to Goldman Sachs and had a variety of roles, including head of UK trading and head of European emerging markets trading, establishing Goldman's euro convertible and European warrants business in London. After twelve years he left for CSFB where he became European head of convertibles and later on managing director in the Leveraged Funds Group Fund. He founded CQS 1999 and serves as chief executive and senior investment officer.

INVESTMENT PHILOSOPHY Hintze has expanded CQS from being a top convertible bond hedge fund to a multi strategy investment management firm. He utilizes a combination of a top down macro thematic analysis and bottom-up fundamental research and integrates diverse areas of knowledge such as macroeconomics, fiscal and monetary policy and geopolitical trends with security selection. It is a complex work – not for amateurs – and it needs interconnection between the different parts of the firm to understand the whole spectrum of the investment in this process. He prefers to be most active in August and around Christmas because that's often the time, he thinks, when great opportunities become available for producing alpha.

OTHER CQS manages over $11 billion (a considerable part of which came from Hintze's former employer at the start). He was, in other words, a star in the investment world even before he started out on his own. He runs multiple strategies in hedge fund and long-only strategies both in bespoke and co-mingled forms. The firm has racked up numerous awards over the years. The ABS Fund has produced annual performance over 29 % since inception in October 2006. Hintze is an active philanthropist and has donated over £30 million to charity. He has interests in a farm in Australia, is known to quote the Bible in public speeches, and speaks fluent Russian.

Sources: Michael Hintze; CQS Directional Opportunities Fund; Wikipedia; Institutional Investor, 2011.

CARL
ICAHN
USA

ANNUAL YIELD
22%
for **22** YEARS
BENCHMARK 10%

There are no words in our vocabulary that define the common quality that all very successful people share, but the closest words would be 'passion' or 'obsession' relating to what they do. A second quality these people share is a lack of hubris when achieving a great victory in a game or investment. When they are victorious they do not believe they are geniuses, rather they understand how much luck is involved. As Rudyard Kipling put it, 'if you can meet with Triumph and Disaster and treat those two impostors just the same'.

A third quality that I believe all great investors share is the ability to recognize the difference between a 'secular and cyclical' change in companies they have carefully studied. If a company they have studied and believe in is down because of a cyclical change, successful investors use the opportunity to purchase as much as they can as quickly as they can. They do not care and are not influenced or frightened by market conditions, etc. However, if a company is in trouble due to 'secular' change, successful investors will take their losses and back away.

The ability to recognize secular and cyclical cycles cannot be taught, in my opinion. Rather, it is an instinct or talent that has been honed over many years of arduous work. In other words, the great investors, just like the great champions in other fields, can divorce themselves from their emotions and just play the game.

BORN New York, USA 1936.

EDUCATION He studied philosophy at Princeton University in 1957 and at the New York University School of Medicine, but he left without graduating.

CAREER Icahn began his career on Wall Street in 1961 as a registered representative with Dreyfus & Company. Aged 32 he bought a seat on the New York Stock Exchange and started Icahn & Co. Inc., a brokerage firm that focused on risk arbitrage and options trading. In 1978, he began taking substantial controlling positions in individual companies. Today, he is chairman of Icahn Enterprises, a diversified publicly listed holding company engaged in a variety of businesses, including investments, metals, real estate, and consumer goods.

INVESTMENT PHILOSOPHY Icahn is the most successful and famous stock market activist in the world, but his roots are in contrarian value investing. His strategy is to invest in beaten-down assets that nobody else wants, usually out of bankruptcy, then fix them up and sell them when they are back in favour. When studying a firm's structure and operations to explore the reasons for any disconnect between the company's stock price and the true value of its assets, 'for the most part the reason for this disconnect is management', as he explains it. To take the steps necessary to seek to unlock value he uses tender offers, proxy contests, and demands for management accountability. When valuing companies, he looks at replacement cost, break-up value, cash flow and earnings power, and also liquidation value.

He operates with almost all market instruments – including long and short equities and bonds, bank debt and other corporate obligations, options, swaps, etc. He regards consensus thinking as generally wrong. 'If you go with a trend, the momentum always falls apart on you' says Icahn. In contrast to the general view about activists, he is more of a long-term investor. The focus is on capital structure, management, and finding the best long-term owner for the assets.

OTHER Icahn Enterprises had 2011 revenues of $11 billion and total equity of $7.8 billion. In 2008, Icahn launched the Icahn Report, which campaigns for shareholder rights and encourages them to shake up the management and boards of underperforming companies. He has through his different vehicles taken positions in various corporations over the years and very seldom failed to wring out changes and higher valuation.

Some of the most famous battles were RJR Nabisco, Texaco, TWA, Phillips Petroleum, Western Union, Gulf & Western, Viacom, Blockbuster, Time Warner, Yahoo, and Motorola. In the fight over Time Warner, where he owned about 3.3 %, he unveiled a 343-page proposal calling for the break-up of the company. In 2012 his net worth was estimated by Forbes to be $14 billion, making him the fiftieth richest man in the world. He has been an active participant in a variety of philanthropic endeavours through Icahn Charitable Foundation, which mainly focuses on child welfare, education, and medicine.

Sources: Carl Icahn; Icahn Enterprises L.P.; Icahn Enterprises; the Icahn Report; Wikipedia.

KENT
JANÉR
SWEDEN

ANNUAL YIELD
12%
for **15** YEARS
BENCHMARK 3%

Successful investors have two important abilities. One is the ability to identify interesting and potentially profitable investments. This is grounded in a well thought-out analysis of macroeconomic developments, a stock, or some other investment. If the market valuation is too high or too low in relation to what the analysis indicates is correct, things become interesting. The probability of finding a good deal increases if you also understand the reasons for this disparity. If, on the other hand, there is no apparent reason for the disparity, there is a greater risk that the market is right, and you have missed something in your own evaluation. Financial prices assume predictions about the future, but predictions are considerably more uncertain that most of us would like to believe. Accepting and locking yourself into a particular scenario that appears to be reasonable right now is not a good way of handling insecurity. It is better to think in terms of a variety of possible future scenarios, weighing up the possibility of them occurring. The market price should then reflect a reasonably balanced assessment of these scenarios. Because new information is forever becoming available, you should adjust your weightings over time, and therefore also what you think a reasonable market price.

The other ability of successful investors is to identify and handle risk, which is mostly aimed at reducing the chances of catastrophic results from your investments. The worst possible result is so bad that you no longer can, may, or wish to make new investments. Rule number one is to never risk ending up in this situation. Further, it is important to understand which risks you are exposed to, and actively decide whether they are the ones you wish to carry, or if there are particular risks that should be insured or protected against. In many cases it can be wise, for the right price, to have a general insurance against unexpected events or macroeconomic shocks. Mathematical models can be very useful for measuring risk, but they should be combined with practical experience of financial markets. Excessive belief in models, which are of course simplifications of reality, can be downright dangerous. Good judgement and common sense are required, both of which are often underappreciated qualities.

If you as an investor want high risk-adjusted returns over a long period of time in a changeable world, you will need to know about financial theory and understand macroeconomic structures and relationships, not to mention politics, including central bank policy-making. Without a certain understanding of these topics (which does not necessarily mean expert knowledge) there is a risk of becoming a one-trick pony, and making the same investment over and over again, despite the fact that reality has changed so that the factors and relationships which ensured success in the past are no longer valid.

Hard work and a passion for what you do are definitely important factors in success!

BORN Laisvall, Sweden 1961.

EDUCATION Janér graduated from the Stockholm School of Economics in 1984.

CAREER His first job after graduating was as a market maker in government bonds for Svenska Handelsbanken. After two years he switched to a similar role at Citicorp in London, working with British gilts. In 1989, Janér started working for the Swedish bank JP Bank with responsibility for bonds and the bank's investment strategy. In 1998 he founded the hedge fund Nektar Asset Management, where he has been head of investments from the start, and is now also chairman of the board.

INVESTMENT PHILOSOPHY Janér runs Nektar, one of the decade's most successful hedge funds in Europe. The fund is market neutral and looks for misvaluations between various financial instruments, which are advantageous from a risk perspective. The positions can also be based upon a macroeconomic theme (lower growth, higher inflation, higher volatility, etc.). The emphasis is on interest rate market. The fund usually holds several hundred positions and is characterized by relatively low risk.

OTHER Janér made his name by being one of the most successful investors to take positions on the falling Swedish krona in 1992. Today, Nektar manages over $4 billion. Among the large number of international awards received over the years, for three years in a row Hedge Funds Reviews named Nektar the best market-neutral fund in Europe over the previous ten years. He is a member of the scientific advisory board of the Stockholm Institute for Financial Research, and his hobby is deep-sea fishing.

Sources: Kent Janér; Nektar Asset Management.

RAKESH
JHUNJHUNWALA
INDIA

INDIA'S WARREN BUFFETT

Ten commandments for investing:
→ Be an optimist! The necessary quality for investing success.
→ Expect a realistic return. Balance fear and greed.
→ Invest on broad parameters and the larger picture. Make it an act of wisdom, not intelligence.
→ Caveat emptor. Never forget this four-letter word: R-I-S-K!
→ Be disciplined. Have a game plan.
→ Be flexible. For investing is always in the realms of possibility.
→ Contrarian investing. Not a rule, not ruled out.
→ It's important what you buy. It's more important than at what price you buy.
→ Have conviction. Be patient. Your patience may be tested, but your conviction will be rewarded.
→ Make exit an independent decision, not driven by profit or loss.

BORN Mumbai, India 1960.

EDUCATION Jhunjhunwala graduated from Sydenham College in 1985 and later became a charted accountant.

CAREER Jhunjhunwala started directly after school to invest on his own account. After a couple of very good years he founded the stock trading firm Rare Enterprise and he is still CEO and the sole owner of the company. He sits on several boards of unlisted and listed companies in India.

INVESTMENT PHILOSOPHY Jhunjhunwala is both a trader and a long-term investor. For the longer-term investing, Jhunjhunwala focus on companies with external competitive advantage, scalability, good management, and an

EVA (profit earned by the firm less the cost of financing the firm's capital) that must remain positive during the investing period. He also takes notice of companies' capital rising. He prefers buying small companies with big potential: companies characterized by low institutional holdings, being under-researched, and surrounded by general pessimism catch his interest. He is careful not to dig too deeply into analysis or, as he himself put it in a recent interview, "I don't believe too much deep analysis is necessary. I don't want to be paralysed by it. All you need is common sense". His short-term trading is influenced by the lessons from George Soros's trading strategies and Marc Faber's analysis of economic history. He endorses the rule of thumb that 'trend is my best friend'. He uses leverage frequently and is regarded on the Indian market as a risktaker.

OTHER Jhunjhunwala is the first investor billionaire in India. So far he has made most money in trading. He started out with $100 and has had an annual return of almost 80 % annually for 27 years. The Indian market has, of course, developed amazingly during this period (25% annually), but this is nevertheless three times better than the index. He has formulated several ethical and investment rules he forces himself to follow. One is 'You cannot make money based on borrowed knowledge'. Recently Jhunjhunwala announced that he will donate around $1 billion to charity by 2020. He has decorated his trading room with quotations from famous investors.

Sources: Rakesh Jhunjhunwala;indiatimes.com; Wikipedia.

BANG-CHUN KANG

SOUTH KOREA

ANNUAL YIELD

16%

for **9** YEARS

BENCHMARK 12%

Focus on the changes. When I make an investment decision, I look at the business environment, for example, demography, consumption trend, infrastructure etc. Among the elements, Currently I am keeping my eye on the changes in leadership structure and industrial structure. The leadership of the world has been replaced as China gains more economic and political power in the world. The economic power transference in the 1930s from Britain to the US is a good example of structural leadership change. The industrial structure also changes. The Industrial Revolution brought about a large reform of society, and the modern industrial society dawned at the beginning of the Industrial Revolution; however, efficiency and profitability of the related industries are gradually decreasing. It is about time for new industry to arise, including green energy and the mobile revolution.

Look at the industry leaders. All industries repeatedly experience periods of ups and downs. I define industry leaders as the great companies that continue to survive through these cycles. Moreover, the business environment keeps changing. You should adhere to the dynamic industry leaders that strengthen their market dominance by actively adapting to change.

Imagine investing based on daily life and understanding of fundamentals. Ponder upon information and experiences that people commonly encounter. Hidden values can always be found in our daily lives. Instead of ending up in mere consumption, take a step further and always question why. For example, why should I pay for the product, and how the company's business model helps to make money in the process. This leap of imagination will enable us to find the great companies hidden in our daily surroundings.

BORN Rural South Korea 1960.

EDUCATION Kang graduated from HanKuk University of Foreign Studies in 1987, having majored in Management Information Systems (MIS).

CAREER Kang began investing professionally at SK Securities in 1987. Since then, he has worked for SsangYong Investment Corp. and Dongbu Investment Corp. as a fund manager. In 1999, aged 39, he set up AssetPlus Investment Advisory, which later turned into his current investment management company. He still serves as chairman.

INVESTMENT PHILOSOPHY Kang is a renowned value investor in South Korea involved only in the stock market and strongly influenced by Graham and Buffett. He looks for strong business models and is notably patient with a long-term investment horizon. Like the classic value investors, he believes that a stock is a tool to becoming involved in great companies.

OTHER Kang has won several awards in South Korea (Outstanding Manager, etc.). His biggest success was investing long term in the stock market crash of 1997. He likes to go cycling in his spare time.

Sources: Bang-Chun Kang; Asset Plus Investment Management.

MARK E.
KINGDON
USA

ANNUAL YIELD
17%
for **30** YEARS
BENCHMARK 10%

→ Cut your losses and let your profits run.

→ You are neither as smart as you (and others) think you are when things go well, nor as dumb as you feel when markets turn against you.

→ Investment management is a wonderful, challenging profession, as long as you keep things in perspective. Maintaining a balanced life that prioritizes family and community service will make you a happier individual and, ultimately, a better investor as well.

BORN New York, USA 1949.

EDUCATION Kingdon received a BA in Economics Phi Beta Kappa from Columbia College and an MBA from Harvard Business School in 1973.

CAREER He started working at AT&T's pension group. After two years he left to join the hedge fund Century Capital Associates, where he became general partner. Aged 34 he founded Kingdon Capital Management where he still serves as president and member of the Executive Committee and Sector Head for Asia, Emerging Markets and Technology.

INVESTMENT PHILOSOPHY Kingdon is a global top-down and bottom-up hedge-fund investor. His is a mix of both fundamental and technical analyses, applied to a global array of stocks, bonds, currencies, commodities, and credits. Global stocks tend to form the largest part of the portfolio. When investing in the equity market, he acts more as a growth investor, regarding earnings momentum as crucial, even if balance sheets are not neglected; however, the sentiment has to be right, and cutting losses is a mantra in the organization, as are liquidity in its positions and sell targets. Another cornerstone is the market's view of the target position in order to monitor the critical variables and remain ahead of the crowd. However, he regards his fundamental research as his edge. The fund holds above 200 equity positions with average holding period of less than one year. He usually does not use leverage.

OTHER Kingdon oversees around $3 billion in assets. In high school Kingdon was already writing an investment newsletter. He serves on the boards of Columbia University, the Harlem Children's Zone, the New York City Police Foundation, the Social Science Research Council and Carnegie Hall. In 2003 he was the recipient of the Institutional Investor/ Alternative Investment News Lifetime Achievement Award. He practises yoga, pilates and taekwando.

Sources: Mark Kingdon; Kingdon Capital; Kingdon Associates Fund; Wikipedia.

SETH A. KLARMAN
USA

ANNUAL YIELD
19%
for **27** YEARS
BENCHMARK 9%

Price is perhaps the single most important criterion in sound investment decision-making. Every security or asset is a 'buy' at one price, a 'hold' at a higher price, and a 'sell' at some still higher price. Yet most investors in all asset classes love simplicity, rosy outlooks, and the prospect of smooth sailing. They prefer what is performing well to what has recently lagged, often regardless of price. They prefer full buildings and trophy properties to fixer-uppers that need to be filled, even though empty or unloved buildings may be the far more compelling, and even safer, investments. Because investors are not usually penalized for adhering to conventional practices, doing so is the less professionally risky strategy, even though it virtually guarantees against superior performance.

Most investors feel compelled to be fully invested at all times – principally because evaluation of their performance is both frequent and relative. For them, it is almost as if investing was merely a game and no client's hard-earned money was at risk. To require full investment all the time is to remove an important tool from investors' toolkits: the ability to wait patiently for compelling opportunities that may arise in the future. Moreover, an investor who is too worried about missing out on the upside of a potential investment may be expose himself to substantial downside risk precisely when valuation is extended. A thoughtful investment approach focuses at least as much on risk as on return. But in the moment-by-moment frenzy of the markets, all the pressure is on generating returns, risk be damned.

You must buy on the way down. There is far more volume on the way down than on the way back up, and far less competition among buyers. It is almost always better to be too early than too late, but you must be prepared for price markdowns on what you buy.

BORN New York, USA 1957.

EDUCATION Klarman graduated in Economics from Cornell University and took an MBA in 1982 at Harvard Business School.

CAREER Klarman first worked one year for the two famous investors Max Heine and Michael Price of the Mutual Shares Fund (now a part of Franklin Templeton Investments). After his MBA he founded the Baupost Group LLC where he is president and portfolio manager.

INVESTMENT PHILOSOPHY Klarman is a risk-averse value investor who takes positions in both private and public assets globally. He operates over a wide array of investments ranging from fairly traditional value stocks to more esoteric investments such as distressed debt, liquidations, and foreign equities or bonds. He specializes in illiquid and complex assets, where fewer investors compete. One of the metrics he focuses on is liquidation value. Complex derivatives, put options, and other intricate tools are often used in the investments. Despite being a hedge fund, he rarely shorts stocks and avoids leverage. He is obsessed with reducing risk and often holds a significant amount of cash in his investment portfolios, sometimes in excess of 50 %. Stocks usually account for a small share of the total. To describe in one word what Baupost works with, it would have to be 'mispricing', due to overreaction. He regards traditional, long-oriented analysis as simplistic, highly optimistic, and sloppy.

OTHER Despite his unconventional strategies with a high proportion of cash, he has consistently achieved high returns. In the last ten years Baupost has beaten S&P500 by roughly 15 percentage points yearly. His risk-adjusted numbers are spectacular; take into account the assets under management – above $24 billion – and they are even more impressive. In a recent letter to his clients he announced that he didn't want to be their highest-achiever fund during one single year – presumably a unique statement in the branch. In 1991, Klarman published Margin of Safety, Risk Averse Investing Strategies for the Thoughtful Investor, which since has become a value investing classic. Now out of print, Margin of Safety has changed hands on eBay for $2,000. He keeps a low profile but is a senior lecturer on value investing at Harvard Business School and involved in a variety of philanthropic activities. He is a fan of baseball and horse racing.

....

Sources: Seth Klarman, *Margin of Safety: Risk-averse Value Investing Strategies for the Thoughtful Investor* (1991); Seth Klarman – Letter to clients of Baupost, 2005, 2008, 2010; Bloomberg BusinessWeek, June 2010; Wikipedia.

EDWARD
LAMPERT
USA

ANNUAL YIELD
29%
for **22** YEARS
BENCHMARK 10%

The idea of anticipation is key to investing and to business generally. You can't wait for an opportunity to become obvious. You have to think, 'Here's what other people and companies have done under certain circumstances. Now, under these new circumstances, how is this management likely to behave?'

One of the things I try to advocate to other investors and companies is that if you can have a large long-term investor then you have the ability to run the company for the long term.

So much time and money ends up spent ensuring that the financial statements are immune from criticism that it can become much more of a distraction than a useful tool for investors and managers.

BORN New York, USA 1962.

EDUCATION Lampert graduated with a BA in Economics from Yale University in 1984.

CAREER After school he started as an intern at Goldman Sachs. Inspired by Warren Buffett's letters to shareholders he left its risk arbitrage department in 1988 to start his own hedge fund ELS aged 26. He still serves as chairman and CEO.

INVESTMENT PHILOSOPHY Lampert defines himself as an 'aggressive conservative' investor; one could also say a 'concentrated value' investor. He is uncommon for a hedge-fund manager in that he is a mix of investor and businessman. He is, among other things, chairman of Sears, the gigantic retailer store. Lampert focuses on finding companies that are seriously undervalued, and he is willing to target poorly run ones because they can produce greater returns if the right changes are made. As a result,

Lampert is more hands-on with management, and the number of invest-ments is normally below ten, although intimately known holdings are kept for several years.

Lampert's style of investment requires a more detailed knowledge of the business, company management, and its values, than those who invest for shorter periods of time. He seems to prefer mature and eas-ily understandable companies that generate lots of cash. He thinks past performance as a measure of quality is wildly overrated. When investing, he focuses intensely on how their companies allocate capital to maxi-mize returns. Lampert has significant experience investing in retail, even if his first retail investment was only in 1997. He does not have any known shorting strategy.

OTHER Lampert has carefully studied Buffett for years. He went back and read annual reports in the couple of years preceding some of Buffett's investments: 'Putting myself in his shoes at that time, could I under-stand why he made the investments?' He has also been nicknamed 'the new Warren Buffett'. Lampert is most famous for forming and merging Kmart and Sears into Sears Holdings. He took control of Kmart (the third largest discount store chain in the US, then with above $20 billion in sales) by buying up debt during its bankruptcy. ELS has around $10 billion in assets under management. Lambert's earnings in 2004 were estimated to be $1.02 billion, making him the first Wall Street finan-cial manager to exceed an income of $1 billion in a single year. Forbes estimated his wealth to be $3 billion in 2011. In 2003 Lampert was kid-napped, but he managed to talk himself out of the situation and was released after two days.

Sources: Edward Lampert; CNNMoney; Bloomberg; Sears annual letter to sharehol-ders, 2008; the Third Avenue Management Investor Conference and Luncheon, 18 November 2003; BusinessWeek, 2007; Wikipedia.

JESSE LIVERMORE
USA

ANNUAL YIELD
55%
for **37** YEARS

→ Never act on tips.

→ Never buy a stock because it has had a big decline from its previous high.

→ If a stock doesn't act right, don't touch it; because, being unable to tell precisely what is wrong, you cannot tell which way it is going. No diagnosis, no prognosis. No prognosis, no profit.

→ Don't blame the market for your losses. Never add to a losing position. A losing position means you were wrong.

→ Stocks are never too high for you to begin buying or too low to begin selling. But after the initial transaction, don't make a second unless the first shows you a profit.

→ Always sell what shows you a loss and keep what shows you a profit.

→ Don't argue with the tape. Do not seek to lure the profit back. Quit while the quitting is good—and cheap.

→ There is only one side to the stock market; and it is not the bull side or the bear side, but the right side.

→ The speculator's chief enemies are always boredom from within.

→ A man must believe in himself and his judgement if he expects to make a living at this game.

→ Bulls and bears make money, but pigs get slaughtered.

→ Markets are never wrong. Opinions are!

BORN Shrewsbury, Massachusetts, USA 1877. Died 1940.

EDUCATION Dropped out of high school.

CAREER At the age of 14 Livermore left the farm where he grew up and hitched a lift to Boston. There he began working in Paine & Webber's Boston brokerage office. He studied price movements and began to trade their price fluctuations. Two years later he quit his job and started to trade on his own. When Livermore was in his twenties, he moved to New York to speculate in the stock and commodities markets. The rest is history.

INVESTMENT PHILOSOPHY Livermore was an autodidact who created his own investment strategy and traded with his own money. He focused on catching the big moves up and down, prudently riding the large trends over time and avoiding trading every minute. Livermore became the first trend follower long before the term existed. Perhaps his most important innovation was his strategy in security trading to increase the size of a position while it was going in the right direction but cutting losses quickly. In addition he also took surprising positions based on fundamental analyses of both companies and the economy at large. He saw every mistake as a way to improve his strategy, or as he wrote: 'There is nothing like losing all you have in the world for teaching you what not to do. And when you know what not to do in order not to lose money, you begin to learn what to do in order to win. Did you get that? You begin to learn!'

OTHER Livermore was probably the greatest stock trader ever, and is certainly one of the most legendary. He was also nicknamed 'the Great Bear of Wall Street'. After 1929 his wealth was estimated to $100 million, or above $2 billion in today's prices. If we assume he started, as he said, with a few dollars, that means an annual return of 55 % for 37 years. He was famous for his memory and mathematic skills, but also for being a secretive loner who disliked distractions – his employees were not allowed to talk during market hours, for example. Livermore was by no means a perfect trader and went bankrupt at least twice, mainly because he ignored his own trading rules. When doing well, he liked to live well, with a handful of houses, several Rolls Royces, a private train carriage, a couple of yachts, and so on. His nominally anonymous biography, Reminiscences of a Stock Operator, went on to become a Wall Street classic and is still the traders' bible. He also wrote How to Trade in Stocks. At the age of 63 he committed suicide after a long struggle with depression.

Sources: Edwin Lefèvre, *Reminiscences of a Stock Operator* (1923); Jesse Livermore, *How to Trade in Stocks: the Livermore Formula for Combining Time Element and Price* (1940); jesse-livermore.com; Wikipedia.

DANIEL
LOEB
USA

ANNUAL YIELD

17.5%

for **16** YEARS

BENCHMARK 5.8%

Many of the boards we have come across are populated by individuals who rely on the stipends they receive from numerous corporate boards and thus appear motivated primarily to ensure continuing board fees, first-class air travel and accommodations, and a steady diet of free corned beef sandwiches until they reach their mandatory retirement age.

I have learned a very painful lesson about investing in less liquid positions. Needless to say, we will not be making these types of investments again.

The only thing we are 100 % confident in is that we are fallible, we don't have all the answers, and we will make some mistakes. However, if we are honest with ourselves and our colleagues, remain attentive to our own biases and deceptions, focus on process, attempt to understand why we erred, and engage in deliberate practice and self-observation to improve our decision-making ability, we will not only minimize our errors, but also ultimately become better people and better investors.

BORN Santa Monica, California, USA 1961.

EDUCATION Loeb graduated in Economics in 1984 from Columbia University.

CAREER He began his career as a lawyer at E. M. Warburg Pincus & Co. After a brief period as a corporate developer at Island Records, Loeb started to work for the New York-based hedge fund Lafter Equity Investors and later moved on to the investment bank Jefferies and Co. to work as an analyst. Before founding the hedge fund Third Point LLC in 1995 he gained further industry experience working at Citicorp as vice-president of high yield sales.

INVESTMENT PHILOSOPHY Loeb is a hedge-fund manager with a strategy best described as event-driven and value-based – nimble, opportunistic, and especially situation-focused. The analyses concentrate on legal, regulatory, and accounting issues. Besides equities, Third Point invests in corporate credit, mortgages, currencies, and commodities, mainly in the US market. He uses a bottom-up analysing approach and puts risk on or off quickly and decisively. Due to his background in bankruptcies he likes to invest in companies in extreme financial difficulties. He spends considerable time thinking about the macroeconomic environment and betting on market direction. In addition, Loeb also uses shareholder activism as a part of the portfolio. His is sometimes a rocky road: in 2008 the fund lost 38 %.

OTHER Third Point is one of the biggest hedge funds, with around $9 billion in assets. Loeb is well known in the financial world for his sharp pen, especially in his public communications expressing his disapproval of the performance and conduct of other financial executives. In a 2005 letter to Star Gas Partners, a fuel distributor, Loeb called its chief, Irik P. Sevin, 'one of the most dangerous and incompetent executives in America'. He has hosted fundraising parties and sits on the boards of Prep for Prep and Third Way, a non-partisan political think-tank. It's said he first became interested in stocks at the age of 5, and actively traded stocks before even graduating from high school. Loeb reportedly enjoys art collecting, yoga, and surfing.

Sources: Daniel Loeb; Third Points quarterly letters; Valuewalk; Wikipedia.

PETER
LYNCH
USA

ANNUAL YIELD

29.2%

for **13** YEARS

BENCHMARK 15.8%

The basic story remains simple and never-ending. Stocks aren't lottery tickets. There's a company attached to every share. Companies do better or they do worse. If a company does worse than before, its stock will fall. If a company does better, its stock will rise. If you own good companies that continue to increase their earnings, you'll do well. Corporate profits are up fifty-five fold since World War II, and the stocks market is up sixtyfold. Four wars, nine recessions, eight presidents, and one impeachment didn't change that.

You don't need to make money on every stock you pick. In my experience, six out of ten winners in a portfolio can produce satisfying result. Why is this? Your losses are limited to the amount you invest in each stock (it can't go lower than zero) while your gains have no absolute limit. All you need for a lifetime of successful investing is a few big winners, and the pluses from those will overwhelm the minuses from the stocks that don't work out.

Nothing has occurred to shake my conviction that the typical amateur has advantage over the typical professional fund jockey.

BORN Newton, Massachusetts, USA 1944.

EDUCATION Lynch graduated from Boston College in 1965 and took an MBA at the Wharton School of the University of Pennsylvania in 1968.

CAREER Lynch started as an intern with Fidelity Investments in 1966, partly because he had been caddying for Fidelity's president, became an analyst, and in 1974 director of research. In 1977, Lynch was named head of the then small and obscure Magellan Fund. Lynch resigned as a fund manager in 1990 to spend more time with his family. Lynch has since taken different positions in Fidelity. At present he is vice chairman.

INVESTMENT PHILOSOPHY Lynch is one of history's most illustrious growth-oriented stock investors. Lynch has invented several new approaches to investing. His most famous investment principle is simply 'Invest in what you know', popularizing the economic concept of 'local knowledge' – investors learn more from visiting the local grocery shop than staring at charts. Another key innovation was PEG (price–earnings ratio compared to growth). Lynch is also considered one of the foremost advocates of GARP (growth at reasonable price), but in well-managed companies with sound balance sheets. He does not care about liquidity in the stock, and prefers small and mid-size companies. He also favours turnaround cases and asset plays. Overall he has a very flexible investment strategy, to the extent of being known as 'The Chameleon'. Companies, which invest in luxury head offices at the cost of returns to shareholders, are never admitted to the portfolio.

OTHER Outperforming the benchmark by over 13 percentage points in 13 years without leverage is probably a record for a mutual fund, especially when value stock performed better than growth stock during the period, and Lynch didn't invest in tech stocks such as Microsoft and Cisco, which were two of the best performing stocks in the market. The Magellan Fund increased from $18 million to $14 billion during his management. When he resigned, Magellan had more than 1,000 individual positions. Lynch recommends investors to stay in the stock market even when times are bad, as the risk of missing the next rally is worse. The only time to prefer other investments is when bonds give more than 6 % higher interest than dividend yield. Lynch is also the inventor of 'ten-baggers'–companies whose value increases tenfold. When managing the fund he read 700 annual reports yearly. He has written three books. Since his retirement, he has been an active participant in a variety of philanthropic endeavours.

Sources: Peter Lynch, *One up on Wall Street* (2000); Fidelity Investments; Magellan Fund; Investopedia.

MIAN MUHAMMAD
MANSHA
PAKISTAN

THE MOST SUCCESSFUL INVESTOR IN PAKISTAN

K eeping in mind the consistent return on equity, it makes sense to invest in products or services that have consistent demand even in a recession. It is easy to be an investor, but one needs a lot of discipline to distinguish between greed and investing.

Invest in projects that serve value to customers and the price serves value to you. A detailed study and analysis can give you that insight.

For beginners, I would suggest a careful diversification for short as well as long periodic revenue together with an eye for capital gain. A seasonal investor must be able to sustain/hold investments even in tough times. Long-term investment always reaps better results. Typically, long term means 1–2 years for normal stock and 4–5 years for strategic stock.

BORN Bangladesh 1947.

EDUCATION Mansha studied accounting at Hendon College, London.

CAREER Mansha started his career in the textile industry in 1969 at Nishat Mill, his family business, which he took over aged 22. He raised its performance beyond all recognition and diversified by investing in other operations including, power, cement, aviation, insurance, and banking. He is the chairman of Nishat Group as well as the chairman and board member of several other listed and non-listed companies and organizations in Pakistan and abroad.

INVESTMENT PHILOSOPHY Mansha is a long-term investor, both in the stock market and beyond. His philosophy is to invest in companies that see stable demand, even in recessions. Market segment and customer base are more important than the company. This is a consistent strategy, with a focus on safe and mature industries that ensures low risk. There are no high-tech initiatives here. For Mansha, the long-term view is central, whether investing in public companies or privately owned, unlisted ones, and thus far the model has borne fruit no matter which sector he has entered.

OTHER Today, Nishat Group consists of twelve companies, including six listed ones, and Mansha is the largest private employer, exporter, and taxpayer in Pakistan. He is also Pakistan's first dollar billionaire, and the richest person in the country, with a personal fortune estimated at $4–5 billion. The media sometimes call him 'Mr Pakistan'. Outside of business, Mansha is involved with philanthropy and enjoys watching cricket.

Sources: Mian Muhammad Mansha; Wikipedia.

ROBERT
MAPLE-BROWN
AUSTRALIA

ANNUAL YIELD
9.5%
for **26** YEARS

BENCHMARK 8.4%

→ Firstly, I am a 'value' investor and I believe that extensive fundamental analysis of each investment is very important.

→ Secondly, although I believe that diversification is important, I believe Australian equity portfolios should only have about thirty individual investments.

→ Thirdly, 'value' is not the same as 'cheap', and so the industry in which the company operates and the quality of its management are all important in determining 'value'.

BORN New South Wales, Australia 1940. Died 2012.

EDUCATION Maple-Brown graduated from the University of New South Wales in 1965 with a degree in Commerce, and become a Chartered Accountant five years later.

CAREER Maple-Brown joined the merchant bank International Pacific Corporation, which later became Rothschild Australia. After being responsible for the investment management division, he left in 1984 to form Maple-Brown Abbott Ltd. aged 44. He was CEO until 2000 and was non-executive chairman until his death.

INVESTMENT PHILOSOPHY Long-term bottom-up value stock picking is probably the best description of Maple-Brown's investment style. Confident that markets are inherently inefficient, he took advantage of inevitable periods of excess pessimism by buying when valuations were depressed and selling when valuations became extended during periods of excess optimism – a contrarian approach. Maple-Brown's investments in general had lower price–earnings ratios, lower valuations of book value, stronger balance sheets, and a higher dividend yield than the market. The focus was on balance sheet strength and by reconciling reported profits with underlying cash flow. He invested in all asset classes, but was famous for his stock market investments and did not back off in case of pushing for changes in management when necessary.

OTHER Maple-Brown's value-based investment philosophy started the tradition of value investing in the Australian market. Adjusted for having around 20 % in cash on average, the fund has beaten the benchmark substantially since its inception, and currently manages in excess of $9 billion. He had the long-term performance record in managing Australian equity portfolios and balanced funds. Maple-Brown was inspired by Benjamin Graham in the 1960s.

Sources: Robert Maple-Brown; Maple-Brown Abbott Pooled Superannuation Trust; Wikipedia.

HOWARD
MARKS
USA

ANNUAL YIELD
19%
for **22** YEARS
BENCHMARK 12%

In order to be a superior investor, you must think differently from – and better than – other investors. I call this 'second-level thinking'. Consensus thinking – 'first-level thinking' – is part of the process through which the mass of investors value assets, and thus it is reflected in the market price of assets at any point in time. It's obvious that in order to be able to identify the instances when market prices are too low, and buy – or too high, and sell – you must out-think the consensus that set the market price. To be a superior investor you must achieve a superior understanding of many things. Here are my candidates for the three most important:

You must understand risk, what it consists of, and the importance of putting top priority on controlling it. You must understand that superior investing results come not just from finding winners, but also from limiting risk by minimizing losers. And you must understand that success in investing comes not from buying high quality assets but from buying things at prices that are low enough to both (a) provide room on the upside and (b) limit the downside in case expectations turn out to have been too rosy. The risk-conscious investor views the future in terms of a distribution of possible outcomes and, in buying, makes allowance for a wide range of scenarios, not just the one he believes to be most likely – which by definition is positive enough to support a 'buy' decision.

You must understand the role in markets played by psychology and herd behaviour. You must understand the importance of controlling the deleterious effect on behaviour of emotion and ego. You must be willing to do several things that are emotionally difficult and uncomfortable: (a) admit to limits on your knowledge and foresight, especially regarding the macro, and reflect those limits in your actions; (b) take contrarian positions that are out of step with the herd; and (c) look wrong during the inevitable periods before your divergent views are proved right. You must be willing to pass on a bad investment that is currently popular and performing well, and unafraid to buy the underpriced gem that nobody else is buying, and thus is languishing.

You must reach a deep understanding of cycles and their history. You must understand that reversion to the mean is usually more likely than the unabated continuation of a trend that has been underway for a while. You must be aware of where we are in the current cycles – political, economic, and market – and behave in a countercyclical fashion. You must refrain from increasing your aggressiveness when things are on an upswing, making it easier to behave aggressively and avoid becoming increasingly cautious in the downswings, which give rise to increasing pessimism and render positive behaviour more challenging. Economics, corporate finance, accounting, financial modelling, and financial statement analysis are essential components in the investment process, and, in general, intelligent people can be taught them. Those nuts and bolts have to be performed competently and, hopefully, in a superior fashion. But that's not enough. Those things are unlikely to lead to success if deep conceptual understanding does not precede them. This is the essential foundation for a superior record.

BORN New York, USA 1946.

EDUCATION Marks holds a B.S.Ec. from the Wharton School of the University of Pennsylvania having majored in Finance. He also hold an MBA in Accounting and Marketing at the Graduate School of Business of the University of Chicago in 1970.

CAREER After sixteen years at Citicorp – first as an equity research analyst and later as senior portfolio manager in charge of convertible and high yield securities – he moved to the TCW Group, where he was responsible for investments in distressed debt, high yield bonds, and convertible securities. Aged 49 he co-founded Oaktree Capital, where he serves as chairman.

INVESTMENT PHILOSOPHY Marks is a bottom-up value investor mainly focusing on debt. Oaktree Capital's strategy is to invest in less efficient markets and alternative investments that have led to corporate and distressed debt, convertible securities, distressed debt, real estate, and emerging market securities. The risk analysis is crucial in the process.

OTHER Oaktree Capital has grown into the biggest distressed-debt investor in the world, with $80 billion in assets. Marks is famous for his memos to clients and he recently wrote the investment book *The Most Important Thing*. He practises yoga and uses diet plans.

Sources: Howard Marks; Oaktree's 17 distressed-debt funds; Bloomberg.

MARK
MOBIUS
HONG KONG/SINGAPORE

ANNUAL YIELD
15%
for **22** YEARS
BENCHMARK 11%

Diversify. It is actually possible to have all your eggs in the wrong basket at the wrong time. To reduce one's vulnerability to this eventuality, every investor should diversify. That is your best protection against unexpected events, natural disasters, and dishonest management as well as investor panic. Moreover, global investing across all sectors is always superior to investing in only one market or industry. If you search worldwide, you will find more bargains and better bargains than by studying one nation. You never want to be overly dependent on the fate of any one stock, market, or sector.

Take a long-term view – investment averaging helps – even if you desire short-term rewards. If you take a long-term view of the markets, you will be less emotional and thus less likely to make careless mistakes, see beyond the short-term volatility of the market, and see patterns of market, political, and economic behaviour that would not be evident to a short-term observer. By looking at the long-term growth and prospects of companies and countries, particularly those stocks, which are out of favour or unpopular, the chances of obtaining a superior return are much greater.

To minimize discomfort or disappointment in the short-term, investment averaging could be undertaken by purchasing consistently in a measured and periodic pattern. Investors who establish a programme from the very beginning, purchasing shares over a set period of time have the opportunity to purchase not only at high prices, but also at low prices, bringing their average cost down.

Accept market cycles – make volatility your friend. Any study of stockmarkets around the world will show that bear or bull markets have always been temporary. It is clear that markets do have cyclical behaviour with pessimistic, sceptical, optimistic, euphoric, panic, and depressive phases. It is this volatility that gives investors the opportunity to sell high and buy low since the manic-depressive nature of markets means that they will rise much more than they should and fall much more than should as well. Investors should thus accept market cycles and plan accordingly.

BORN New York, USA 1936.

EDUCATION Mobius earned his BA and MA from Boston University and his Ph.D. in Economics and Political Science from MIT in 1964. He also studied at Kyoto University in Japan.

CAREER Mobius started working at the international securities firm Vickers-da-Costa, and later was president of the International Investment Trust Company in Taipei, Taiwan. He then ran an independent consulting company prior to joining Franklin Templeton Investments in 1987 as president of the Templeton Emerging Markets Fund. He is currently executive chairman of the emerging markets group and directs analysts based in Templeton's seventeen emerging markets offices, and manages more than sixty portfolios.

INVESTMENT PHILOSOPHY Mobius could be described as a bottom-up value investor. He and his team use in-depth company research to find undervalued securities that have the potential to increase in value over time. He searches for the best investments across all emerging market countries and sectors, aiming to hold investments for at least five years. He also compares the company to its local, regional, and industry peers. Quantitative as well as quality factors are an important function of his study, which involves evaluating financial data going back five years as well as five years of projections. This is usually followed by a company visit, since Mobius is a firm believer in 'kicking the tyres'. He is known as one of the pioneers of emerging markets investment.

OTHER Mobius was named one of the named one of the 'Top 100 Most Powerful and Influential People' by Asiamoney and 'Ten Top Managers of the 20th Century' in a survey by the Carson Group in 1999. He has also received numerous 'Manager of the Year' awards. He has written eight books, including a graphic autobiography, *Mark Mobius – An Illustrated biography of the Father of Emerging Markets Funds.*

Sources: Mark Mobius; Templeton Emerging Market Investment Trust NAV.

CHARLES
MUNGER
USA

ANNUAL YIELD
24%
for **14** YEARS
BENCHMARK 6%

I f you're going to be an investor, you're going to make some investments where you don't have all the experience you need. But if you keep trying to get a little better over time, you'll start to make investments that are virtually certain to have a good outcome. The keys are discipline, hard work, and practice. It's like playing golf – you have to work on it.

You need a different checklist and different mental models for different companies. I can never make it easy by saying, 'Here are three things'. You have to derive it yourself to ingrain it in your head for the rest of your life.

The ethos of not fooling yourself is one of the best you could possibly have. It's powerful because it's so rare.

BORN Omaha, Nebraska, USA 1924.

EDUCATION After studies in mathematics at the University of Michigan he entered Harvard Law School, and graduated 1948.

CAREER He founded and worked as a real estate attorney at Munger, Tolles & Olson LLP until 1965. Before taking up his present role as vice-chairman of Berkshire Hathaway Corporation and 'partner' to Warren Buffett, he managed Wheeler, Munger, and Co., an investment partnership, between 1962 and 1975.

INVESTMENT PHILOSOPHY Munger is a stock market value investor, but has a more flexible approach than the common value investor. He is a supporter of operating with multiple models depending on circumstances. If the investor manages a small number of assets he should search for small cap in leading market positions. In Berkshire Hathaway he has to focus on big companies. If your goal is to become rich quickly you need leverage

– a rule he himself applied in the early stages – but his most famous characteristic is his skill to buy and hold good companies, or as he describes it himself, 'Over the long term, it's hard for a stock to earn a much better return than the business which underlies it earns. If the business earns 6 % on capital over forty years and you hold it for that 40 years, you're not going to make much different than a 6 % return even if you originally buy it at a huge discount. Conversely, if a business earns 18 % on capital over twenty or thirty years, even if you pay an expensive looking price, you'll end up with a fine result.' This strategy explains much of Berkshire Hathaway's fabulous performance. He regards the risk as the most important priority, and he recommends that all investment evaluations should begin by measuring risk, especially risk that could impact on your reputation. Other principles include: (i) Incorporate an appropriate margin of safety. (ii) Avoid dealing with people of questionable character. (iii) Insist upon proper compensation for risk assumed. (iiiv) Always beware of inflation and interest rate exposures. (v) Avoid big mistakes; shun permanent capital loss.

In the end, it comes down to Munger's most basic guiding principles, his fundamental philosophy of life: Preparation, Discipline, Patience, and Decisiveness.

OTHER Munger has introduced the concept of 'elementary, worldly wisdom', a set of mental models answering business-related problems that have influenced the management of Berkshire Hathaway as well. He is an advocate of wisdom, and has said that nothing has served him better in his long life than continuous learning. Not surprisingly, universities are the main beneficiaries of his philanthropy. Two other cornerstones in his work are incentives and ethical issues: he believes that incentives explain why people behave the way they do, and good businesses are ethical businesses. A business model that relies on trickery is doomed to fail. Munger has studied Albert Einstein, Charles Darwin, and Isaac Newton, but Benjamin Franklin is the one he admires most.

Sources: Charles Munger, *Poor Charlie's Almanac* (1978), Charles Munger, "The art of stock picking"; Wheeler, Munger & Co. Partnership; Wikipedia.

JOHN
NEFF
USA

ANNUAL YIELD

13.7%
for **31** YEARS

BENCHMARK 10.6%

onventional wisdom suggests that, for investors, more information these days is blessing and more competition is a curse. I'd say the opposite is true. Copying with so much information runs the risk of distracting attention from the few variables that really matter. Because sound evaluations call for assembling information in a logical and careful manner, my odds improve, thanks to proliferating numbers of traders motivated by tips and superficial knowledge. By failing to perform rigorous, fundamental analyses of companies, industries, or economic trends, these investors become prospectors who only chase gold where everyone else is already looking. Mutual fund investors who think they can make money by chasing the hottest fund are panning the same overworked streams.

Many circumstances and yardsticks have changed. Companies cited have grown, merged, or, in some cases, closed their doors. Dividend yields are not so lavish nowadays, and erstwhile P/E ratios seem almost quaint. Brief security analyses are not intended as current recommendations, but as testimony to the thought processes that shaped Windsor's fortunes. Are they still valid? I think so. The relationship of total return to the P/E ratio still governs my investment decisions, and the returns meet my high standards.

If a lesson emerges besides the merits of low P/E ratios, it should be that successful, long-term investment strategies need not rest on a few very risky glamour stocks. The record will show that we painted our canvas using a broad palette. At various times, Windsor owned representatives of all but two industries, and many were revisited more than once. Some payoffs were of the championship variety; others were nothing to be proud of. Now and then, we hit home runs, but our scoring relied chiefly on base hits. To go home winners, that's all investors need.

BORN Wauseon, Ohio, USA 1931.

EDUCATION Neff graduated summa cum laude with a BA from the University of Toledo in 1955. He obtained his MBA from Case Western Reserve University in 1958.

CAREER Neff started as a securities analyst with the National City Bank of Cleveland 1955. He joined the Wellington Management Co. in 1964, becoming the portfolio manager of the Windsor, Gemini and Qualified Dividend Funds. He retired in 1995 after more than three decades.

INVESTMENT PHILOSOPHY Neff's investment strategy was in reality a blend of contrarian, growth and value investing. He calls himself a low price–earnings investor. He focused on the least popular stocks, but they needed to have an organic growth in excess of 7 %, yield protection, and be a solid company. Investments were always based on rigorous fundamental analysis, examining both management and the books in detail. Future earnings were everything and he regards ROE (return on equity) as the most important single yardstick of what management has accomplished for shareholders. On average, Neff's stocks had a P/E ratio that was half that of the rest of the market. The number of holdings was rarely under 100. He was known for his discipline and his long working days, and for being highly knowledgeable about the companies he invested in.

OTHER The Windsor Fund was the best performing mutual fund during his tenure and became the largest fund, closing to new investors in the 1980s. Of the 31 years he managed the fund, he beat the market in 22 years. He was said to take all the week's Wall Street Journal copies home for a second read over the weekend.

Sources: John Neff, *John Neff on Investing* (2001); CFA Institute; Wikipedia.

KERR
NEILSON
AUSTRALIA

ANNUAL YIELD
11.7%
for 16 YEARS

BENCHMARK 3.3%

There are clearly many ways of taking opportunities that markets present, but the recurring behavioural tendency that we try to exploit is investor's persistence in over-emphasizing the recent event. Though one likes to believe that markets are rational and the world around one is orderly, the reality is probably the very opposite. When something untoward occurs, this is most unsettling to investors and they tend to overreact. This invariably offers wonderful opportunities for those willing to take a different course. An everyday example of this phenomenon was the collapse of air travel immediately after 9/11, even though it was arguably one of the safest times to fly. Another tendency that causes investors mischief is to extrapolate enthusiastically. One can recall the pallet-load of books on Japanese business supremacy at the peak in 1990, and yet all of that is now forgotten, and today we are extrapolating the demise of this nation epitomized by many stocks selling at less than their cash and investment value, i.e. no value placed on their underlying and profitable businesses, and the market as a whole selling at only book value. This clearly is an opportunity for independent-thinking investors.

The greatest problem facing any analyst/fund manager is that we are invariably voyeurs and heavily influenced by the PR machine of the entity we are examining. The creation of this 'energy shield' is exacerbated by the hunger of the media for celebrity and glitz. When an entity reaches an exalted position on the list of the nation's most admired companies, that is precisely when one should be on one's guard and seek out non-corroborative evidence. There are numerous examples of this exalted status being matched by overpriced valuations for companies such as Coca-Cola, GE, Sony, and, more recently, Toyota. (Building new flash headquarters and a CEO addicted to the adoration of the press are as reliable signs of internal rot as you are likely to get.) We have always found the trends will surprise us for their durability. The mistake we have often made is dismissing the slogan in the early days as being nothing more than that. What come to mind here are the over-used sayings of the 1980s and 1990s, like 'shareholder value' and 'sweating the balance sheet'. These movements persisted much longer than we would have believed, and in the case of 'shareholder value', was really code for the subterfuge of transfer-ring partial ownership from shareholders to company management via stock options, in some cases on an extraordinary scale.

BORN Johannesburg, South Africa 1949.

EDUCATION Neilson graduated with a BA in Commerce from the University of Cape Town, South Africa, in 1971.

CAREER He began his career in London working for Courtaulds Pension Investments in 1971, and moved back to South Africa in 1974 where he established a research department for Anderson Wilson in equities research. He moved to Australia in 1984 to work with Bankers Trust, where he ran the retail funds management division. In 1994, aged 44, he founded Platinum Asset Management, a specialist international equity manager. He is still the chief investment officer.

INVESTMENT PHILOSOPHY Neilson is a contrarian stock market value investor. He looks for good, out-of-favour, undervalued equities in all major geographical markets for long-term holdings. Before investing he requires contextual understanding of the company's place in its industry. This obviously requires a good understanding of the industry, the principal competitors, and the personality of individual companies. The most important valuation parameter is the company's intrinsic value. From time to time he uses shorting as a protection. His present portfolio consists of 150 different positions.

OTHER Neilson established Platinum with support from George Soros. He manages at present around $16 billion. His best investment to date is accumulating a lot of Peruvian shares when the terrorist organization the Shining Path was attempting to take control of Peru. Forbes recently estimated his wealth to be $2.4 billion, which places him among the ten wealthiest Australians. Neilson started to invest in the stock market at the age of 13. He has been called by commentators 'the Warren Buffett of Australia'. His hobby is modern Chinese art.

Sources: Kerr Neilson; Platinum International Fund; Fairfax Media; Wikipedia.

WILLIAM J.
O'NEIL
USA

ANNUAL YIELD
40%
for **10** YEARS

When I started investing, I made most of the same mistakes you've probably made. But here's what I've learned:

You buy stocks when they're on the way up in price, and not on the way down. And when you buy more, you do it only after the stock has risen from your purchasing price, not after it has fallen below it.

You buy stocks when they're nearer to their highs for the year, not when they've sunk lower and look cheap. You buy higher-priced, better-quality stocks rather than the lowest-priced stocks.

You learn to always sell stocks quickly when you have a small 7 or 8 per cent loss rather than waiting and hoping they'll come back. Many don't.

You pay far less attention to a company's book value, dividends, or PE ratio – which for the last 100 years have had little predictive value in spotting America's most successful companies – and focus instead on vital historically proven factors such as strong earnings and sales growth, price and volume action, and whether the company is the number one profit leader in its field with superior new products.

You don't subscribe to a bunch of market newsletters or advisory services, and you don't let yourself be influenced by recommendations from analysts or friends who, after all, are just expressing personal opinions that can frequently be wrong and prove costly.

You almost must acquaint yourself with daily, weekly, and monthly price and volume charts – an invaluable tool the best professionals wouldn't do without, but amateurs tend to dismiss as irrelevant.

Lastly, you must use time-tested sell rules to tell you when to sell a stock and take your worthwhile gains. Plus you'll need buy and sell rules for when it's best to enter the general market or sell and lower your percentage invested. Ninety per cent of investors have neither of these essential elements.

BORN Oklahoma City, 1933.

EDUCATION O'Neil took a degree in Business Administration at Southern Methodist University in 1955.

CAREER Aged 25 he started his career as a stockbroker at Hayden, Stone & Company. He bought a seat on the NYSE aged 30 (then the youngest ever to do so). In 1963 he founded William O'Neil + Co. Inc., a company which developed the first computerized daily securities database, and currently tracks over 200 data items for over 10,000 companies. In 1984, O'Neil made research from his database available in print form with the launch of Investor's Business Daily, a national business newspaper. O'Neil still serves as CEO of William O'Neil & Co., is chairman and publisher of Investor's Business Daily.

INVESTMENT PHILOSOPHY O'Neil relies on a mixture of quantitative and qualitative criteria to pick stocks. On the qualitative side he is a growth investor, only focusing on companies with at least 25 per cent earnings growth, and only then if they are leaders in the field. The key idea is to seek out only those growth stocks that have the greatest potential for swift price rises from the moment you buy them. In essence, buy the strong, sell the weak. He thinks diversification is a sign of ignorance. His is a time-consuming style with high turnover due to the principle of selling when losses are above 7–8 per cent. The later approach is based on his belief that the market is always smarter than you. On the basis of his quantitative research, he also takes a strong view on the market. In contrast to, for example, Peter Lynch, who thinks you should always own stocks, O'Neil leaves the market from time to time. He has no approach for short selling.

OTHER He is famous for turning $5,000 into $200,000 in one year (1963). He was a pioneer of database-driven stock selection. His forty years of studying stock-winners illustrates great stocks have seven common performance characteristics before they make major price moves. Those seven criteria are known as 'CAN SLIM'. Investor Business Daily has over one million readers. He has written three books.

....

Sources: William O'Neil, *How to make money in stocks* (2009); Wikipedia.

JAMES P.
O´SHAUGHNESSY
USA

ANNUAL YIELD
10.1%
for **9** YEARS
BENCHMARK 5.3%

The four horsemen of the investment apocalypse are fear, greed, hope, and ignorance. Note that only one, ignorance, is not an emotion. Investor's emotional responses to short-term market conditions are responsible for greater losses than any recession or bear market. The only way to succeed is to conquer your emotional responses to market conditions. Train yourself to be fearful while the majority are greedy, and aggressive when the market is fearful.

Test your investment strategy over the longest period of data you can find – only use strategies that have withstood the test of time and done well over a variety of investment cycles. You would not go to a doctor who gave you a medication simply because it worked on his last five patients. You would demand that the doctor could prove over multiple years and patients that

the treatment worked. Demand the same from your investment philosophy. Insist on empirical proof that your investment strategy is superior and then stay the course.

Give your portfolio an annual check-up. If your asset allocation is 60 % stocks and 40 % bonds, and you find that your current allocation is 40 % stocks and 60 % bonds because of market movement, reset your allocation to your target. It is perhaps the most simple thing to expose, and one of the most difficult to do, because it will force you to take money away from an asset class that has been doing well in the short-term and reallocate to one that has been doing poorly, yet it is one of the single best things an investor should do for the long-term. Remember that you feel day-to-day, yet if you can overcome short-term emotions, your long-term results will be vastly better.

BORN Saint Paul, Minnesota, USA 1960.

EDUCATION O'Shaughnessy has a BA in Economics from the University of Minnesota.

CAREER After graduating, O'Shaughnessy started to work for a family-owned venture capital firm. Aged 28 he launched O'Shaughnessy Capital Management, Inc. He joined Bear Stearns with his team in 2001, but reached a timely agreement with the investment bank to spin his team out to form O'Shaughnessy Asset Management (OSAM) in 2007, with the entire portfolio management team and records in place. He serves as chairman and CEO as well as chief investment officer.

INVESTMENT PHILOSOPHY O'Shaughnessy is both a research guru and a pioneer of quantitative equity money management. He has back-tested 90 years of stock market data to apply empirical, fundamental research to uncover the best quantitative stock-selection strategies. He found that the best performance came from a portfolio with a combination of: 'Quality Companies with Superior Valuation, Momentum, and Yield'. The composition and ranking are computed in a mechanical and unemotional way. Some of the cornerstones and observations based on his study are: (i) Buying recent winners has proven itself over more than 80 years to be one the most effective stock-selection strategies. Stocks with strong momentum consistently outperform the market with less risk. (ii) Price-earnings ratios aren't the best indicator of a stock's value. Cash flow is a better predictor of a stock's future. (iii) Avoiding companies with excessive debt helps to avoid lower performing stocks with higher risk levels. (iv) Stocks with strong yield (dividends and repurchase of shares) consistently outperform the market with less risk. (v) Well-priced value stocks consistently outperform the market with less risk. (vi) The rate at which a growth stock's earnings grow is not as important as the persistence of growth over time.

O'Shaughnessy runs a concentrated portfolio of 25 stocks and is always fully invested. All portfolios and strategies have performed substantially better than benchmarks since OSAM started in 2003. It is most important, he means, to 'consistently, patiently, and slavishly stick with a strategy, even when it's performing poorly relative to other methods'.

OTHER OSAM manages approx. $4.4 billion. O'Shaughnessy is the author of four books on investing. In 2004 he was named 'Manager of the Year' and in 1999 he became the first person to be granted a patent in investment strategy.

....

Sources: James P. O'Shaughnessy; OSAM, All Cap Value 2003–2011; James O'Shaughnessy, *What works on Wall Street* (1998); Wikipedia.

CHETAN
PARIKH
INDIA

ANNUAL YIELD
25%
for **10** YEARS
BENCHMARK 19%

Diligence, discipline, patience, and temperament are vital to good investing. They're easier said than done. Diligence comes from exceptional homework and curiosity; discipline comes from focus on the investment process and detachment from the outcome; patience comes from viewing investing as part ownership in a company, and thus usually ignoring market noise; and temperament comes from not being envious of others and not being greedy.

Buying with a margin of safety is the only anchor against the uncertainty, unknowability, and unpredictability of tomorrow. It is especially true in situations where government policies, corporate and managerial actions, and technological changes can suddenly impact fundamental values.

What can go wrong is a more important question for an investor than asking what can go right. At the heart it is about having manageable downsides, attractive risk–reward ratios, and avoiding permanent losses of capital.

BORN Ahmedabad, India 1957.

EDUCATION He holds an MBA in Finance from the Wharton School of Business and a B.Sc. in Statistics & Economics from the University of Bombay.

CAREER Parikh started work at Indo-Pharma, a family-owned pharmaceutical firm. Aged 35, he founded Jeetay Investments where he serves as chairman and portfolio manager.

INVESTMENT PHILOSOPHY He is a long-term stock market value investor. No effort is put into macro economy or stock market sentiment; his are pure, bottom-up analyses in search of securities trading at significant discounts to their intrinsic value. The true value is for him the present value of the future cash flows. He requires a price quoting at a discount of at least

60 % to the intrinsic value. The lack of opportunities sometimes leaves the fund with a high proportion of cash. On average, the cash level has been around 25 % since inception. The investment horizon is 3–5 years and the portfolios normally consist of no more than twenty positions. The investment targets preferably have a high franchise value and entry barriers, and must be businesses he and his team understand. In order to get the whole picture, Jeetay meets every possible associate of the company, including vendors, customers, middle management, bankers, competitors, etc. In ranking, the importance of the balance sheet comes first followed by the cash flow statement and the profit and loss account. In addition he has a window for 'special situations' such as mergers and acquisitions, restructuring troubled companies, and spin-offs. The primary aim, he says, is to ensure safety of capital.

OTHER Parikh has been rated as one of India's best investors by Business India and been a long-standing columnist in the financial press. He recommends meditation as a means of self-improvement in investing.

Sources: Chetan Parikh; Jeetay Investments; Forbes.

RICHARD
PERRY
USA

ANNUAL YIELD
13%
for **24** YEARS
···········
BENCHMARK 9%

Richard Perry's investment aphorisms:
- → Every investment should be measured on an expected value basis – how much can I make, how much can I lose, and what are the probabilities associated with each outcome.
- → Don't listen to what people say or write, try to intuit what they mean.
- → Good investors use a combination of brains and gut. To paraphrase Leonardo Da Vinci, one must understand the science of art and the art of science.
- → By the time your analysis is perfected the investment opportunity is probably gone.
- → There are many different investment strategies. Focus on the ones you do best and avoid the ones you do poorly.
- → Value is buying a dollar for 50 cents and having a business plan that turns that 50 cents back into a dollar. Value traps are buying a dollar for 50 cents and a business plan that makes that dollar worth dramatically less than 50 cents.
- → People will behave as they are incented to behave.
- → Translate complex theories into simple statements.
- → Beware of obsolescence.
- → Sales and marketing are critical components of a successful business.
- → Invest like a local.

BORN Los Angeles, USA 1955

EDUCATION Richard Perry has a BA from the University of Pennsylvania's Wharton School in 1977, and an MBA from New York University's Stern School of Business in 1980.

CAREER Perry began his career at the options trading desk at the investment bank Goldman Sachs in the mid-1970s. When he left in 1988 to start the hedge fund Perry Capital he was working in equity arbitrage, while lecturing on finance at the Stern School of Business at New York University. He has been CEO of Perry Capital from the start.

INVESTMENT PHILOSOPHY Perry could be described as an event-driven, value-oriented, multi-strategy hedge-fund manager. He controls a number of strategic positions simultaneously, and bases his business model on having several different income streams. One strategy is to seek out companies that have the potential to restructure through acquisitions or disposals, often those in reconstruction after bankruptcy. Another area is investments in distressed loans. However, he also invests in unlisted companies and property, and uses his cash supply to lend money at high returns to investors who are not able to lend from banks. He usually works with a neutral portfolio and with lending. He has called his approach 'expected value analysis': it is based on calculating the percentage likelihood of various outcomes and multiplying them by the current bond price, after which he compares the expected value with the current market price to determine whether he should buy or sell. Every now and again he becomes deeply engaged with a particular investment. Recently, he became the principal owner of Barneys New York, a luxury American chain store.

OTHER At present Perry manages $8 billion in assets. For the first 19 years, his hedge fund did not have a single deficit year. Perry was also one of a few on Wall Street to start betting against subprime mortgages as early as 2006. He is the chairman of the board of Barneys New York Inc. and a member of the boards of trustees of Facing History and Ourselves. His mentor at Goldman Sachs was Robert Rubin, US Secretary of the Treasury during the Clinton administration. Perry is an avid collector of pop art and a triathlon runner.

Sources: Richard Perry; Perry Capital.

T. BOONE
PICKENS
USA

THE WORLD'S GREATEST OIL INVESTOR

Chief executives, who themselves own few shares in their companies, have no more feeling for the average stockholder than they do for baboons in Africa. Always keeping in mind that shareholders are the owners of a company, while members of the management are employees.

Far too many executives have become more concerned with the four P's – pay, perks, power, and prestige – rather than making profits for shareholders.

Show up early, work hard, stay late. Work eight hours and sleep eight hours, and make sure they are not the same eight hours.

BORN Oklahoma, USA 1928.

EDUCATION Pickens graduated from Oklahoma A&M (now Oklahoma State University) with a degree in geology in 1951.

CAREER He started his career at Phillips Petroleum in 1951. In 1956 he founded the company that would later become Mesa Petroleum, which turned into one of the world's largest independent oil companies. In the 1980s, Pickens became famous as a corporate raider, with several big deals of which Gulf Oil was among the largest. By the mid-1990s he gave up his raiding after a brutal and expensive fight with Unoca. In 1997 Pickens founded BP Capital Management. He holds a 46 % interest in the company, which runs two hedge funds, Capital Commodity and Capital Equity.

INVESTMENT PHILOSOPHY Pickens is an oilman and shareholder activist who in later years has become a hedge-fund manager. He is entirely concentrated on the energy sector, mostly in oil. His analysis starts at the top, with a scenario for the different forms of energy, from where he drills down to the individual company. He prefers to seek out badly run companies where he can influence their governance and management. In his role as a hedge-fund manager he has a different strategy to his earlier days, when he was an activist and would even buy whole companies (in those days there were many deals which never came to fruition, but with enough noise and fuss the stock rose nevertheless and Pickens was able to exit with excellent profits).

Pickens's key characteristics as an investor are his knowledge of the energy sector, endurance, and courage. He is possibly the most risk-inclined investor in this book. One example is how through his company Mesa Petroleum he bought the thirty-times larger Hugoton Production. His hedge funds are not for the weak of heart either. One of them was founded in 1997 and lost 90 % in two years. The other hedge fund showed an annual return of 38 % for six years, before becoming one of the greatest loss-makers in the sector in 2008. Pickens's reckless style is perhaps best described in his own words in a quotation from Katherine Burton's book *Hedge hunters*: 'Most of my ideas work, but the timing gets screwed up every once in a while.'

OTHER He was involved in the creation of the United Shareholders Association. Pickens has been outspoken on the issue of peak oil, and advocates alternative and renewable energy sources such as solar and wind. Pickens owns more water assets than any other individual in the US. In 2007 Pickens earned $2.7 billion as the Capital Equity Fund increased 24 % after fees, and the $590 million Capital Commodity fund grew 40 %. Pickens has donated more than $700 million to charity. According to Forbes he is "only" worth 1.6 billion US dollars today.

Sources: T. Boone Pickens, *The First Billion is the Hardest* (2008); Katherine Burton, *Hedge hunters: After the Credit Crisis, How Hedge Fund Masters Survived* (2007); boonepickens.com; Businessweek; Insider Monkey; CNBC.

MICHAEL F.
PRICE
USA

ANNUAL YIELD

20%

for **21** YEARS

BENCHMARK 10%

O riginal sources of information: these have to be non-inside, but especially with the Internet there is ample opportunity to develop sources that are unique. Street research is worthless and a waste of time. You are better off reading 10-Q's.

The better the input, the better the odds; in other words keep digging, because your competitors are.

Portfolio structure: never borrow money, always try to have cash as ammu-nition, and I like a mix of two-thirds deep value, mostly small- and mid-cap, one-third cash, plus special situations such as liquidations, merger arbitrage, and bankruptcy investing.

Doing work on these areas keeps your pencil sharp. You must be willing to have conviction about your work as to asset values, and buy when others are selling without respect to asset value.

BORN New York, USA 1953.

EDUCATION Price earned a BBA from the University of Oklahoma.

CAREER He began his career in 1973 when he joined the renowned value investor Max Heine as a research assistant at Mutual Series. Aged 35 he became president, chairman, and owner of the whole company. He increased the assets by more than $17 billion. In 1996 he sold Mutual Series to Franklin Templeton Investments. He left Franklin Templeton in 2001 to begin his own fund, MFP Investors LLC.

INVESTMENT PHILOSOPHY Price is a stock value investor, but with wider repertoire than the common run of value investors. His style also includes taking stakes in bankruptcies and mergers. One of his key strategies is to buy enough shares to give him the clout to force a merger or a turnaround, often using the media to increase the pressure. He does not estimate intrinsic value based on discounted future earnings, as he views that process too difficult; instead, Price likes to compute intrinsic value using what smart investment banks pay for companies after doing a great deal of due diligence. His main focus is on original research by talking to customers and competitors as well as reading all relevant information from annual reports, trade data, and merger proxies to bankruptcy disclosure documents, etc. He looks for evidence of change – new management, restructuring, restatements, acquisitions, failed deals, lawsuits. The method is a time-consuming one.

Companies in a bankruptcy process or in major restructuring effort often need a cash injection. Price usually injects cash into these companies, giving them a breathing space, and then profits from their eventual turnaround. The strategy often ends up with smaller, undervalued, and temporarily out-of-favour stocks.

OTHER Price is a Wall Street icon and was elected one of the ten most successful investors of the twentieth century. The legendary investor Seth Klarman (p. 132) credits Michael Price with being one of his main mentors. His present investment vehicle, the private firm MFP Investors, has $1.6 billion under management, most of it his own money. Price is an active philanthropist, mainly through his foundation the Price Family Foundation, which offers grants to individuals and households going through financial hardship. He has also donated tens of millions of dollars to his alma mater. He is a football fan and a beekeeper.

Sources: Michael Price; MFP Investor; Michael Price lecture at the Columbia Business School, 2006; Mutual Shares Fund; Wikipedia.

THOMAS ROWE
PRICE
USA

ANNUAL YIELD

15%

for **40** YEARS

BENCHMARK 8%

It is better to be early than too late in recognizing the passing of one era, the waning of old investment favourites and the advent of a new era affording new opportunities for the investor.

Change is the investor's only certainty. Changing social, political and economic trends as well as trends of industries and companies require change in the selection of shares in business enterprises.

Every business is manmade. It is a result of individuals. It reflects the personalities and the business philosophy of the founders and those who have directed its affairs throughout its existence. If you want to have an understanding of any business, it is important to know the background of the people who started it and directed its past, and the hopes and ambitions of those who are planning its future.

Buy stocks of growing businesses, managed by people of vision, who understand significant social and economic trends and who are preparing for the future through intelligent research and development.

BORN Linwood, Maryland, USA 1898. Died 1983.

EDUCATION Price graduated from Swarthmore College with a degree in chemistry in 1919.

CAREER After a very brief stint as a chemist Price started working with the brokerage firm of Mackubin Goodrich. Price eventually rose to become its chief investment officer. He founded T. Rowe Price 1937 and sold the company 1965. He remained the company's CEO until his retirement in 1971.

INVESTMENT PHILOSOPHY Price was a long-term growth stock investor. He looked for companies whose earnings and dividends could be expected to grow faster than inflation and the overall economy. The focus on identifying well-managed companies in interesting sectors with good prospects for the long term was virtually unheard of at the time. Discipline, process consistency and fundamental research became the basis for his investments. John Train, author of *Money Masters of Our Time*, says that Price looked for these characteristics in growth companies: superior research to develop products and markets; a lack of cutthroat competition; comparative immunity from government regulation; low total labour costs, but well-paid employees; and at least a 10 % return on invested capital, sustained high profit margins, and a superior growth of earnings per share.

Another criterion was that the company should have doubled its profits in the previous ten years. Price and his partners held on to the stocks as long as earnings continued to grow. That was why he held Black & Decker for 35 years. If these companies showed signs of maturing and profits stagnated, Price would sell immediately. The heart of Price's growth stock investing strategy was the belief that stocks went through several phases; growth, maturity and decline. Even if he followed strict investment rules he changed strategy when needed. When traditional growth stocks began to be overvalued, he moved over to small-cap growth stocks – but the requirement for growth remained the same. There was a contrarian element to his approach. He was said to have a gift for seeing around the next corner, and the intelligence to tailor his investment strategy to whatever came next.

OTHER Price is known as 'the father of growth investing'. His was the first company to charge fees based on the assets under management instead of charging a commission. Price started his first mutual fund in 1950 and provided investors with the best ten-year performance of the decade. He wrote a private booklet for his friends and family entitled 'A Successful Investment Philosophy Based on the Growth Stock Theory of Investing', later published, in which he tried to convince investors that you do not need to know a lot about stocks to be successful. Price was extremely disciplined and organized. He still got up at 5 a.m. when he was in his eighties, and he followed a minutely planned timetable every day.

....

Sources: John Train, *Money Masters of Our Time* (2000); New York Times; Investopedia; Wikipedia.

MIKAEL
RANDEL
DENMARK

ANNUAL YIELD
10%
for **20** YEARS
BENCHMARK 5%

→ Invest with a long-term perspective in well-run companies with a sustainable business model that generates free cash flow for the owners. Make sure you understand the company and the underlying factors driving growth so you understand when your assumptions change. These companies you can keep during bad times and they will come back. That way you exploit the power of a compounded interest rate.
→ Work with a risk level that suits you.
→ Be certain you understand where your risk level really is. Think independently and try to get early into well-run companies with good long-term structural growth opportunities. Don't underestimate the power and longevity of structural trends.

BORN Boden, Sweden 1942.

EDUCATION Randel holds a M.Sc. from the University of California, Los Angeles, and an MA from Lund University, Sweden.

CAREER Randel started as an analyst at Aktiv Placering (a subsidiary of SEB) in 1969, where he ended up as portfolio manager. In 1979 he became CFO at the Federation of Sweden Farmers (LR). Back to SEB in 1982 he took up a position as a managing director of Skandifond, managing international equities. In 1986 he co-founded Carnegie Asset Management and became CEO. He was a portfolio manager for Carnegie Worldwide Global Equities from the start, and retired at the end of 2011.

INVESTMENT PHILOSOPHY Randel is a global, long-term, analysis-led, value-based investor in the stock market. He is strongly of the opinion that long-term investments are an essential factor in achieving high returns over time. What distinguishes Randel from other value investors is his use of global and structural trends as a tool in choosing stocks. The goal of this trend-based stock picking is to identify those companies with the best long-term growth in their cash flow. The companies selected by this model often have new products on the market and increase both their sales and their margins for several years.

Evaluating the free cash flow is a key element upon which Randal places great weight, but his preferences shift according to the look of the business model. If the company uses its initial profits to lower prices so as to increase market share at low margins, cash flow can give the wrong signal. Randel believes that sales growth and gross margin in that case are more important parameters. For him, the most important thing is to understand the company's business model. He is an advocate of concentrated portfolios with at most thirty holdings.

OTHER Randel is the most prominent and successful stock market investor in Denmark. He spends his spare time reading history, and economic history in particular.

Sources: Mikael Randel; Carnegie Asset Management.

JULIAN
ROBERTSON
· USA

ANNUAL YIELD
25%
for **20** YEARS
BENCHMARK 14%

Be confident with what you are investing in and do not expect too much right away; get in there and start trying.

You sell a stock when it's reaching your objectives, and if you are dead wrong you should certainly sell. I do not use stop losses. I've got my targets and do not need them to be out there for the whole world to play against.

We had wonderful analysts who took me from being a cheap-scale investor—one who bought on the basis of assets—to kind of a growth investor, because I could count on a long period of time, and that was a better way to invest if you really know you could get the growth.

BORN Salisbury, North Carolina, USA 1932.

EDUCATION Robertson graduated in Business Administration from the University of North Carolina at Chapel Hill in 1955.

CAREER After military service, Robertson started as a stockbroker for Kidder, Peabody & Co. He stayed for 22 years and eventually became head of the firm's asset management division (Webster Securities). Aged 47, after a sabbatical year in New Zealand, he launched the hedge fund Tiger Management Group with an initial investment of $8 million in assets. He returned the money to external investors in 2000 and continued to manage his own money in the fund as well as financing upcoming hedge fund managers, in return for a stake in their fund management.

INVESTMENT PHILOSOPHY Robertson is an analysis-driven hedge fund king with emphasis on the stock market. His style is somewhat difficult to define and as time has passed it has moved on from focusing on values to more growth. The Tiger philosophy was to use intensive research to identify stocks of solid companies to buy and bad companies to short. Robertson described his style thus: 'Our mandate is to find the 200 best companies in the world and invest in them, and find the 200 worst companies in the world and go short on them. If the 200 best don't do better than the 200 worst, you should probably be in another business.' He is known for taking big bets when he is confident. His investment style also included the competitive drilling of analysts in an idea-pitching process, forcing them to defend the cases; he constantly pressed the analysts to replace good ideas with even better. In addition, Robertson has uniquely intuitive sense, some kind of financial DNA, which is tricky to replicate. Over time he has become more focused on macro as well as growth stocks. He also invests in other assets than stocks. In 1996 he made a fortune by shorting copper.

OTHER By the mid-1990s Tiger Management had over $21 billion in assets under management, by that time the largest hedge fund in the world. Unconvinced by the dot-com rally, Tiger Management put in a negative performance in 1998 and was down 19 % in 1999. Robertson went private with the fund in April 2000, just as the dot-com bubble burst, and paid back money to the investors. Robertson's nickname is the 'Wizard of Wall Street'. Various interviews and articles indicate that Robertson has performed on average above 30 % annually on his private account since 2000. Around a hundred current hedge fund managers got their start at Tiger Management. Robertson has financed most of these hedge funds. Known as Tiger Cubs, they are in general very successful. That makes Robertson by far the most connected and influential individual in the hedge fund community. Robertson is known for handling columns of numbers in his head, but also for having difficulty remembering people's names. Robertson is an active philanthropist and serves on a number of organization and university boards. He is a keen golfer and spends half his time in New Zealand where he has had a golf course built.

Sources: Julian Robertson; Julian Roberson and Daniel A. Strachman, *A Tiger in the Land of Bulls and Bears* (2004); Tiger Management; Lois Peitz, The New Investment Superstars (2001); Bloomberg; Absolutreturn-alpha.com; Wikipedia.

BRUNO
ROCHA
BRAZIL

ANNUAL YIELD
30.18%
for **30** YEARS
BENCHMARK 13.3%

As this book shows, there are many different ways to succeed in investing. At Dynamo, we have always been bottom-up fundamental investors. The insights below have been provided in the context of what worked for Dynamo since we started in 1993 in Brazil:

While there are many investors who would claim they invest with a long-term perspective, very few actually do. It is really difficult to think and invest with a long-term view. First, there are the pressures of the industry. Almost every investor looks at returns on a calendar year basis. Most performance fees are paid on annual basis and so are bonuses at investment firms. It is tough to think on a multi-year basis.

Second, an investment manager can only really think and invest long term if his clients think the same way. It is not easy to find these clients. Thirdly, if an investment manager does not trade often, it seems like he is not doing his job (especially if short-term results are not good). There is an imperative to act, to have new ideas, to sell poor performing stocks, etc.

Finally, our brains are not really wired for long-term investing. We find it hard to

value events that will happen in more than a few years out. And probably more importantly, long term is boring; nothing happens most of the time whereas short term is exciting, gets the adrenaline rushing.

If you really want to invest with a long-term perspective, you will have to do a lot of your own research because you need to have a very strong opinion about the companies in your portfolio. Conviction is key to withstanding market volatility, which is, by definition, much greater than the volatility of business fundamentals. The objective should be to know more about the business than any other outsider. Crucial.

And you will only truly understand a business when you have seen it through good and bad times; there are no shortcuts. On the other hand, knowledge does not depreciate; you can keep accumulating it forever.

Having deep knowledge about businesses is what creates the level of conviction necessary to build a concentrated portfolio, which is what generates outperformance.

Long-term results will be better (and you will have more fun) if you can work with a group of people who you like and admire, whose skills complement one another's, who share the same values, and who enjoy what they do.

Not that one needs to have Asperger's Syndrome to be a good long-term investor, but it helps if one is more interested in reading annual reports (and the notes to financial statements) than in following daily market action. It would have been impossible for Dynamo to succeed if the partners did not have this kind of personality.

BORN Rio de Janeiro, Brazil 1961.

EDUCATION Degree in Economics from the Catholic University in Rio de Janeiro, 1982.

CAREER Rocha started as a trader at Banco Garantia, the most successful investment bank in Brazil. He also worked in corporate finance and spent three years abroad, in London and New York. He left the bank in 1992 and went on to found Dynamo, together with Pedro Eberle, in 1993.

INVESTMENT PHILOSOPHY He is a long term, research-driven, stock market value investor. Key issues are market position, pricing power, discipline in capital allocation, and free cash flow. All investment decisions at Dynamo are made by consensus.

OTHER Rocha now operates out of London where he is responsible for the international fund at Dynamo. Luiz Orenstein, with whom Rocha has shared the responsibility of running the firm since 1997, is the senior partner overlooking operations in Brazil on a daily basis. His hobbies are tennis and football.

Sources: Bruno Rocha; Dynamo.

ROBERT L.
RODRIGUEZ
USA

ANNUAL YIELD
15%
for **25** YEARS
BENCHMARK 9%

R ead history, read history, read history, as conveyed to me by Charlie Munger in Professor Guill Babcock's investment course 37 years ago. This served me very well through countless panics and recessions.

Buy them when they hate 'em and sell them when they love 'em. Being a dedicated contrarian investor is easy in theory but difficult in practice. The crowd always has good reasons for why you are wrong.

Homework, homework, homework. Discipline, discipline, discipline. The power of knowledge about your investments places you at a decided advantage to most, and not letting your emotions get the better of you is critical in achieving superior investment results.

BORN Los Angeles, USA 1948.

EDUCATION Rodriguez, a CFA, received a BBA and an MBA, both from the University of Southern California.

CAREER He started his investment career as an investment analyst at Transamerica Investment Services in 1971. After 10 years, he left to become vice-president and senior portfolio manager in the Chairman's Department of Kaufman & Broad, Inc. Rodriguez joined First Pacific Advisors in 1983 and is now a managing partner and CEO.

INVESTMENT PHILOSOPHY Rodriguez is a long-term stock and bond market value investor. He takes a contrarian approach to investing, and believes that investment opportunities are created when fear and panic are present. He prefers investing in small and mid-sized companies, but it must be an understandable and successful business. His five criteria for searching for stocks are: (i) Leadership positions and a history of profitability.

(ii) Balance sheets with little leverage. (iii) Management teams of high quality. (iv) Potential for profitability improvement. (v) Prices at least 50 % below what he believes the business is worth today.

Absolute rather than relative value is critical. On average, his investments have lower P/E and price–book value ratios than average, stronger balance sheets, and free cash flow with improving returns on equity. His investment outlook is typically 3–5 years, and he is not afraid to sit on the sidelines while waiting for the right opportunity. Rodriguez usually holds between 25 and 35 stocks, while packing up to 40–50 % of assets into the top ten positions.

OTHER FPA Capital Fund was the number one diversified equity fund in the US for 25 years to 2009. FPA New Income, which he also manages, is the only domestic bond fund never to have had a negative year. He pinpointed the coming 2008 financial meltdown in May 2007. Rodriguez supervised approximately $6 billion in 2009 and has been recipient of Morningstar's 'Mutual Fund Manager of the Year' a number of times. His hobby is racing Porsches.

Sources: Robert L. Rodriguez; First Pacific Advisors; FPA Capital Funds; Wikipedia.

JIM
ROGERS
SINGAPORE

ANNUAL YIELD

45%

for **10** YEARS

BENCHMARK 4%

Stay with things about which you yourself know a great deal. Do not rely on others unless and until you yourself are very knowledgeable about the investment.

The best opportunities are often in areas which are ignored. They are often ignored because things have been going wrong for some time, which usually makes them cheap as well. Positive change usually comes eventually, so if you can see it before others, you will be successful. A combination of very cheap and positive change usually leads to positive secular changes which can last for years. The more you are ridiculed and ignored, the more likely you are to be correct. If you are wrong, you will mainly lose opportunity costs. Likewise, shorts come from the reverse. Looking at things which are extremely popular are also things which are usually very expensive. Never short something just because it is expensive, because they often get more expensive. Wait until you see the negative, secular changes (which always come) on the horizon, then act. You will certainly be even more scorned when you point out the looming problems of a popular sector, so be sure you have done your homework so you have the mental staying power.

Do nothing most of the time. Just wait until you see money lying over in the corner. Then go over and pick it up. Be careful after it works out (if it does), because then you will be most cocky and think you are smart since you will have made so much money. Beware of hubris and a feeling that you have to jump back in immediately. Go to the beach for a while and look out the window while you calm down.

BORN Baltimore, Maryland, USA 1942.

EDUCATION Rogers graduated with a BA in History from Yale University and acquired a second BA degree in Philosophy, Politics, and Economics from Balliol College, Oxford in 1966.

CAREER After serving as an analyst for a couple of investment companies he ended up in 1971 at Arnhold and S. Bleichroeder, where he met George Soros and later cofounded the Quantum Fund. He retired in 1980, aged 37, to become private investor. Since then Rogers has served as a professor at Columbia University, financial commentator, author, and adventurer.

INVESTMENT PHILOSOPHY He is a contrarian investor, strongly believing that the market is nearly always wrong. He makes few moves and has long investment horizon. Even if he is well known for his commodity focus and skills, he is more of a globally omnivorous investor, making bets on macro, countries, and almost all asset classes. One of his preferred investing environments is when markets are hysterical for some reason – but they must be fundamentally sound before he takes action. He regards the commodity market as the best investing market on the long side these days. As a private investor, he constantly analysed the countries through which he travelled for investment ideas. He invested in India before its markets were opened to foreigners and turned a huge profit when they were. Rogers calls his style 'Local, wherever I am'.

OTHER As early as 2002 he saw the real estate and consumer debt bubbles coming. In 2006, Rogers said he was shorting US financials, homebuilders, and Fannie Mae. George Soros described him, in one of his books, as 'an outstanding and extremely hardworking analyst, doing the work of six'. He is the creator of the Rogers International Commodities Index (RICI). In 1990–92, Rogers fulfilled a lifelong dream: motorcycling 100,000 miles across six continents. Ten years later he travelled for three years, passing through 116 countries. He has three Guinness records (two from travelling) and has written five books. In 2007 he moved to Singapore and is quoted as saying: 'If you were smart in 1807 you moved to London, if you were smart in 1907 you moved to New York City, and if you are smart in 2007 you move to Asia'.

Sources: Jim Rogers; George Soros, *Soros on Soros: Staying Ahead of the Curve* (1995); Quantum Fund; Wikipedia.

JOHN
ROGERS
USA

ANNUAL YIELD
10.7%
for **26** YEARS
BENCHMARK 8.8%

With nearly 30 years working in the market, I have tremendous respect for just how efficient it is. Increasingly, I think the only way to beat the market is to think independently to find the few opportunities it offers. Going along with the crowd doesn't work, and even paying too much attention to conventional wisdom – which is often groupthink – will make it very difficult to achieve outstanding results.

Investing demands that you focus on the long term, even though most market participants are increasingly focused on the short term. The short term is noise, the long term is signal.

Investors should only buy what they understand. Whether you are talking about an individual company or a stock mutual fund, if it does not make good sense to you, you are likely to sell at the wrong time due to confusion or fear.

BORN Chicago, USA 1958.

EDUCATION Rogers graduated in economics from Princeton University in 1980.

CAREER After graduating he worked as a stockbroker at the investment bank William Blair & Company in Chicago. In 1983, at the age of 24, with the financial backing of family and friends, Rogers started his own firm Ariel Capital Management (now Ariel Investments, LLC). He is the chairman and CEO of the company as well as its chief investment officer.

INVESTMENT PHILOSOPHY As a value-oriented investor, Rogers originally had the simple idea of identifying undervalued small and medium-sized stocks with a proven ability to grow over the long-term, and then holding them until they reached full value, which turned out to mean four or five years. This was a tactic that worked then, and still works now. He believes that patience, independent thinking, and a long-term outlook are essential to achieving good returns. His fund seeks to purchase companies whose prospects allow for double-digit cash earnings growth with a low valuation relative to potential earnings. The P/E multiple should be less than 13 times forward cash earnings and/or a 40 % discount on the intrinsic value (counted as private market value PMV), or the price a professional investor would be prepared to pay for the whole company. In addition he also requires several parameters of quality in the process. The company should have high barriers to entry, sustainable competitive advantages, and predictable profit levels.

OTHER Roger's passion for investing started when he was 12 years old, and instead of toys his father bought him stocks every birthday and Christmas. Since 2001, he has written a regular column, 'The Patient Investor', for Forbes magazine.

Ariel Investment has close to $5 billion in assets under management and is the largest minority-run mutual fund firm in the US. Its logo is a turtle, and the company slogan is 'Slow and steady wins the race'. Ariel runs an academy for children in one of the most deprived communities in Chicago.

Beyond Ariel, Rogers serves as a board member of McDonald's Corporation and is a director of the Robert F. Kennedy Center for Justice and Human Rights. Following the election of President Barack Obama, Rogers served as co-chair for the Presidential Inaugural Committee in 2009. He is a former basketball player.

Sources: John Rogers; Ariel Investments; Wikipedia.

CHARLES M.
ROYCE
USA

ANNUAL YIELD

12.4%
for **30** YEARS

BENCHMARK 9.8%

→ We are risk managers first and foremost.
→ You cannot eat from the table of relative returns.
→ Bad business models can't be cured by valuations.

BORN Washington DC, USA 1939.

EDUCATION He received a BA in Economics from Brown University and an MBA from Columbia University.

CAREER Prior to founding Royce & Associates in 1972 at the age of 32, Royce was director of research at Scheinman, Hochstin, Trotta, a brokerage firm. He was also a security analyst at Blair & Co. for a spell. Royce remains president and CEO of Royce & Associates, and is still portfolio manager for several funds in the group.

INVESTMENT PHILOSOPHY Royce is a disciplined small cap long-term value stock investor. His is a bottom-up investment approach looking for high quality companies with the potential for a successful future that have the following characteristics: strong balance sheets: high internal rates of return; and the ability to generate free cash flow and dividends.

He bases his assessment of a company's value on either what he believes a knowledgeable buyer might pay to acquire the company or what he thinks the value of the company should be in the stock market. Mid-2012 the average position was valued at 1.8 times book value, and had a trailing price earnings multiple of 14.7, as opposed to 15.3 for the Russell 2000 Index.

Unlike most other small-cap investors, Royce is not focused on growth companies. The typical target is a high quality smaller company that is cheap because of cyclical or temporary company-specific issues, often an obscure small cap in a mundane market with a good track record. Further, he prefers to buy into companies whose management has been in place five years or more. The average holding horizon of a position is three to five years.

Royce's is a very demanding strategy in both time and effort. A great deal of time is spent interviewing senior management as well as customers, suppliers, and competitors. Royce tries to reduce the risk by owning a wide variety of stocks, across many sectors and industries.

OTHER Despite the long period in question – fully 40 years – the fund has far outperformed the benchmark (Russell 2000) in every single short- and long-term time frame, an impressive achievement considering assets under management now amount to roughly $40 billion. Royce made recently a $5.5 million gift to his alma mater, Brown University, to fund six professorships. He is engaged in several philanthropic projects as well as the restoration and preservation of landmark buildings. He belongs to the Episcopalian Church and always wears a bow tie.

....

Sources: Charles M. Royce; Royce Pennsylvania Mutual Fund; The Royce Funds; Forbes.

WILLIAM J.
RUANE
USA

ANNUAL YIELD
15%
for **36** YEARS
BENCHMARK 11%

Buy good businesses. The single most important indicator of a good business is its return on capital. In almost every case in which a company earns a superior return on capital over a long period of time it is because it enjoys a unique proprietary position in its industry and/or has outstanding management. The ability to earn a high return on capital means that the earnings which are not paid out as dividends, but rather retained in the business, are likely to be reinvested at a high rate of return to provide for good future earnings and equity growth with low capital requirement.

Buy businesses with pricing flexibility. Another indication of a proprietary business position is pricing flexibility with little competition. In addition, pricing flexibility can provide an important hedge against capital erosion during inflationary periods.

Buy net cash generators. It is important to distinguish between reported earnings and cash earnings. Many companies must use a substantial portion of earnings for forced reinvestment in the business merely to maintain plant and equipment and present earning power. Because of such economic under-depreciation, the reported earnings of many companies may vastly overstate their true cash earnings. This is particularly true during inflationary periods. Cash earnings are those earnings which are truly available for investment in additional earning assets, or for payment to stockholders. It pays to emphasize companies which have the ability to generate a large portion of their earnings in cash.

Buy stock at modest prices. While price risk cannot be eliminated altogether, it can be lessened materially by avoiding high-multiple stocks whose price–earnings ratios are subject to enormous pressure if anticipated earnings growth does not materialize. While it is easy to identify outstanding businesses, it is more difficult to select those which can be bought at significant discounts from their true underlying value. Price is the key. Value and growth are joined at the hip. Companies that could reinvest at 12 per cent consistently with interest rate at 6 per cent deserve a premium.

BORN Chicago, USA 1925. Died 2005.

EDUCATION Ruane graduated from the University of Minnesota in 1945 with a degree in electrical engineering and a Master's from Harvard Business School in 1949.

CAREER After one year at General Electric he went to work for Kidder Peabody, where he stayed for 20 years. Aged 45, Ruane founded his own investment firm, Ruane Cunniff, with partner Rick Cunniff, and the same year they launched their flagship Sequoia Fund.

INVESTMENT PHILOSOPHY As a student and disciple of value investment guru Benjamin Graham, his profile as a stock market investor is obvious. In addition to the above 'insights' it is worth mentioning his meticulous attention to detail. He needed to understand a company and therefore had no taste for tech stocks. The Sequoia Fund today holds a moderately diversified portfolio of 75 positions, both large and small caps. Average holdings are around three years.

OTHER He met Warren Buffett at an investment seminar with Benjamin Graham and he and Buffett became lifelong friends. Most of their customers came to Ruane Cunniff on Buffett's recommendation. Ruane also served on numerous boards, including those of Geico, Data Documents Inc. and the Washington Post. He was a great philanthropist and adopted a block in Harlem, renovating buildings and establishing clinics and community service programmes. He also funded educational programmes on Indian reservations, and supported mental health charities. In addition, he set up TeenScreen, a nationwide organization that tests teenagers for symptoms of depression and other suicide risk factors. Humour and concern for others was his mantra.

Sources: Ruane's 'Four rules of smart investing' from his lecture at Columbia University, compiled by Brian Zen; Life in legacy; Wikipedia.

THOMAS A.
RUSSO
USA

ANNUAL YIELD
14%
for **25** YEARS
BENCHMARK 10%

B y investing heavily in the future, a company can build dominance in their industry. This dominance helps the company to gain competitive advantages. If a company does not invest into the future, it will have problems with competition down the line. Of course, investing in the future may compromise the company's short-term profit. But in the long term, if the company makes right investment decisions, it will have much higher earnings.

One of the lessons I took from Warren Buffett years ago was to define the areas you're comfortable with and stick to them. Branded consumer businesses are those for which I have a natural affinity and that I think I understand. While I would have a hard time on the weekend observing what DRAM chip is in the cellphone of the person walking next to me, I pay a lot of attention to – and think I learn a lot from – what people are wearing, or eating, or smoking, or drinking. Of course these are also all businesses that lend themselves to the types of global growth opportunities I most value.

Jean-Marie Eveillard used to talk about the importance for investors to have the 'capacity to suffer', and I'd argue that same capacity to accept short-term pain for long-term gain is critical in management. The market often doesn't like any burden on reported profits, so adequate levels of investment often invite scorn and ridicule that leaders have to be able and willing to endure. I often find it in family-controlled companies, where management is far more likely to think generationally rather than focus on how to deliver results within some finite period to maximize the value of their stock options. It doesn't require family ownership to find managers who care about their company's future beyond them, but it is even rarer without it.

If you're looking for businesses that will have the highest probability developing emerging markets or taking advantage of traditional markets abroad, my feeling is just, by comparison, that I prefer to find those global leaders abroad.

As an investor in businesses which generate enormous cash flows, my single most important issue to get right is what management will do with cash flow through reinvestment. Do they care about the owner, or do they care about themselves? That's the number one thing.

BORN Janesville, Wisconsin, USA 1955.

EDUCATION Russo has a bachelor's degree in history from Dartmouth College (1977) and an MBA/JD from Stanford University (1984).

CAREER Upon graduation from Dartmouth, Russo served as a fixed income analyst. After his MBA/JD he worked first at Sequoia Fund for four years before joining Gardner Russo & Gardner as a partner in 1989.

INVESTMENT PHILOSOPHY Russo is a long-term value-oriented global equity investor with a somewhat unique investment style. He seeks companies with global brands and with significant growth potential in emerging markets. Appealing consumer brands should give the impression to consumers that there is not an adequate substitute, which makes them aspirational and affords their owners valuable pricing power. Russo's targets also possess a high capacity for reinvestment and are run by management with capacity to suffer short-term pain to deliver long-term gain. High return on invested capital, strong cash flow, and strong balance sheets also typify his portfolio companies. He has focused on the food, beverage, tobacco, and media industries. Regarding valuation, Russo is comfortable holding the right companies with P/E multiples up to the mid-teens. He hopes to invest in attractive companies at a sufficiently wide discount from intrinsic value that the compound growth rate in intrinsic value will deliver a high margin of safety. He has a very low turnover of the portfolio – Nestle, Philip Morris and Heineken have been in the portfolio since 1989. Around 70 % of the holdings are in foreign companies and the top ten holdings account for more than two-thirds of his portfolio.

OTHER Russo has over $6 billion in assets under management. A talk given by Warren Buffett to his Stanford Business School investments class in 1984, where Buffett drove home the importance of focusing on what you know and stretching your investing horizon to allow for companies to compound value, has been of importance in his work. Russo's hobbies are tennis, skiing, travel, and art.

....

Sources: Thomas A. Russo, Value Investor Insight; Gardner Russo & Gardner; Semper Vic Partner Fund.

WALTER J.
SCHLOSS
USA

ANNUAL YIELD
20.9%
for **44** YEARS
BENCHMARK 11.5%

→ Price is the most important factor to use in relation to value.

→ Try to establish the value of the company. Remember that a share of stock represents a part of a business and is not just a piece of paper.

→ Use book value as a starting-point to try and establish the value of the enterprise. Be sure that debt does not equal 100 per cent of the equity. (Capital and surplus for the common stock).

→ Have patience. Stocks don't go up immediately.

→ Don't buy on tips or for a quick move. Let the professionals do that, if they can. Don't sell on bad news.

→ Don't be afraid to be a loner, but be sure that you are correct in your judgement. You can't be 100 per cent certain, but try to look for the weaknesses in your thinking. Buy on a scale down and sell on a scale up.

→ Have the courage of your convictions once you have made a decision.

→ Have a philosophy of investment and try to follow it. The above is a way that I've found successful.

→ Don't be in too much of a hurry to see. If the stock reaches a price that you think is a fair one, then you can sell, but often because a stock goes up say 50 per cent, people say sell it and button up your profit. Before selling, try to re-evaluate the company again and see where the stock sells in relation to its book value. Be aware of the level of the stockmarket. Are yields low and P–E rations high? Is the stockmarket historically high? Are people very optimistic?

→ When buying a stock, I find it helpful to buy near the low of the past few years. A stock may go as high as 125 and then decline to 60 and you think it attractive. Three years before the stock sold at 20, which shows that there is some vulnerability in it.

→ Try to buy assets at a discount rather than buy earnings. Earning can change dramatically in a short time. Usually assets change slowly. One has to know much more about a company if one buys earnings.

→ Listen to suggestions from people you respect. This doesn't mean you have to accept them. Remember it's your money and generally it is harder to keep money than to make it. Once you lose a lot of money, it is hard to make it back.

→ Try not to let your emotions affect your judgement. Fear and greed are probably the worst emotions to have in connection with purchase and sale of stocks.

→ Remember the work compounding. For example, if you can make 12 per cent a year and reinvest the money back, you will double your money in 6 years, taxes excluded. Remember the rule of 72. Your rate of return into 72 will tell you the number of years to double your money.

→ Prefer stock over bonds. Bonds will limit your gains and inflation will reduce your purchasing power.

→ Be careful of leverage. It can go against you.

BORN London, UK 1916. Died 2011.

EDUCATION Schloss did not attend college, but attended courses given by the famous investor Benjamin Graham at the New York Stock Exchange Institute. In 1963, he became a CFA.

CAREER Schloss started on Wall Street in 1934, at the age of 18, at Carl M. Loeb & Co. His teacher Benjamin Graham hired him in 1946. Schloss started his limited partnership in the middle of 1955. His son Edwin joined the partnership in 1973 and the fund changed its name to Walter & Edwin Schloss. Schloss closed his fund in 2000 when he could not find any cheap stocks. He stopped actively managing other people's money in 2003.

INVESTMENT PHILOSOPHY Schloss is a value investor as well as a notable disciple of the Benjamin Graham School of investing. He has a contrarian profile, preferring to invest in stocks that are hitting new lows, often by lacklustre type. But it must be at a low book value, with simple capital structure and a long history. Schloss is focused on assets not earnings. He chooses not to talk to management teams, but needs to see the directors own a fair amount of stock. He is comfortable investing in old industries, avoiding bonds and investing overseas. His strategy is to find stocks that are protected on the downside and then the upside takes care of itself. Schloss relies on the annual reports and is less interested in the nature of business. He does not take the macro or future into account in his investment decisions. The investment must be justified the way they are, not the way they may be in the future.

OTHER Schloss worked out of a small office without any computer, secretary, clerk or bookkeeper. Warren Buffett wrote about his friend in his letter to shareholders in 2006, 'When Walter and Edwin were asked in 1989 by Outstanding Investors Digest, 'How would you summarize your approach?' Edwin replied, 'We try to buy stocks cheap'. So much for Modern Portfolio Theory, technical analysis, macroeconomic thoughts and complex algorithms.' Schloss has more or less the same long track record as Warren Buffett and is, before fees, roughly on par in terms of performance with the Oracle of Omaha. He committed considerable capital to Freedom House, an international NGO supporting democracy, political freedom, and human rights round the world.

Sources: Walter Schloss, 16 Golden Rules of Investing; Warren Buffett's letter to shareholders 2006; Forbes Magazine, 11 February 2008; Walter Schloss's presentation at Benjamin Graham's School of Value Investing, 2006. Wikipedia.

VAN
SCHREIBER
USA

ANNUAL YIELD
16%
for **25** YEARS
BENCHMARK 9%

→ The most important thing in investing is to recognize major trends in the market, positive or negative, early in their development. Then give them a chance to play out. Being on the right or wrong side of a trend can make heroes out of fools or fools out of heroes.

→ Next in importance is competitive advantage. Make sure the company that you are investing in has a clear edge. Cheap valuation matters very little if the company is falling behind its peers. The leaders exert relentless pressure.

→ Cut your losses and let your winners ride. No one is always right, so face up to poor decisions and sell when you have misjudged. On the other hand, do not sell long-term winners simply because they have continued to go up. Be quick to eliminate losers and embrace winners.

BORN New York, USA 1939.

EDUCATION Schreiber has an undergraduate degree from Williams College and received his MBA from New York University.

CAREER He began his career at C. J. Lawrence in 1965 as a research analyst. Later on he became portfolio manager with Deutsche Morgan Grenfell/C.J. Lawrence Inc. Aged 56 he co-founded Bennett Lawrence Management LLC, where he is chief portfolio manager and managing member.

INVESTMENT PHILOSOPHY Schreiber is a domestic growth stock market investor. He searches out companies with competitive edge and profitable growth. Compared with the benchmark of 14, the price-earnings multiple in his fund could be twice the market but also with twice the growth. His portfolio never consists of more than 35 mid-cap companies and he tries to enter the trends, in terms of major demands, early. In addition he uses non-traditional sources of information (consultations with industry leaders, forensic accounting, and risk consulting services) to generate an informational edge.

OTHER Schreiber runs a small boutique investment firm with less than $1 billion in assets under management. When not researching the global markets and individual companies, his hobbies include reading, golfing, and fishing.

Sources: Van Schreiber; Bennett Lawrence Management.

ED
SEYKOTA
USA

ANNUAL YIELD
95%
for **12** YEARS

→ The markets are the same now as they were five or ten years ago because they keep changing – just like they did then.

→ If you want to know everything about the market, go to the beach. Push and pull your hands with the waves. Some are bigger waves, some are smaller. But if you try to push the wave out when it's coming in, it'll never happen. The market is always right.

→ The elements of good trading are cutting losses, cutting losses, and cutting losses. If you can follow these three rules, you may have a chance.

BORN The Netherlands 1946.

EDUCATION Seykota earned a B.Eng. in Electrical Engineering from MIT and a B.Sc. in Management from the MIT Sloan School of Management, both in 1969.

CAREER He started at Commodities Corporation, a privately owned commodity-trading company. In 1970 he pioneered systems trading by using early punched card computers to test ideas about trading the markets. Later on, the brokerage house adopted his system for their trades. Soon thereafter he decided to venture out on his own and manage a few of his clients' accounts. Like many other traders he started to lose money, in Seykota's case in silver.

INVESTMENT PHILOSOPHY Seykota is a commodity trader and a fervent believer in trend following. He regards the fundamentals in traditional research as useless, as the market has already discounted the price – he calls them 'funny-mentals'. He works with small bets risking a maximum of 5% per position and views the temptation to play 'catch up' with the market or instrument as lethal. He does not have any magic formula. The difference is the way he thinks, which boils down to discipline and patience. In a YouTube music video –'The Whipsaw Song' – he discloses his six rules: ride your winners, cut your losses, manage your risk, use stops, stick to the system, and file the news.

OTHER The performance is given in parentheses as the figures cannot be confirmed and he has not been available to participate in the book. According to Future Magazine the performance is above 60 % after fees over three decades. Seykota runs around sixty trading tribes round the world that he supports through blogs and visits. When advising the tribes, he includes mentality training with hypnosis and the like. He has served as a teacher and mentor to some great traders as well. What makes Seykota especially unique is his continual self-examination and commitment to studying the psychological components of trading while also helping other traders achieve their potential. He never advertises his services and has always been very selective about taking on clients. He plays the banjo.

Sources: Jack D. Schwager, *Market Wizards* (1988); Robert Koppel, *The Intuitive Trader: Developing Your Inner Trading Wisdom* (1996); Sunny J. Harris, *Trading 102: Getting Down to Business* (1996); TurtleTrader; Wikipedia.

JAMES H.
SIMONS
USA

ANNUAL YIELD
38%
for **20** YEARS

BENCHMARK 11%

→ There is no real substitute for common sense except for good luck, which is a perfect substitute for everything.

→ Statistic predictor signals erode over subsequent years; it can be five years or ten years. You have to keep coming up with new things because the market is against us. If you don't keep getting better, you're going to do worse.

→ The most important issue is to hire great people because they do a first-class job, offer people great infrastructure, have an open atmosphere and get people compensated on the overall performance.

BORN Newton, Massachusetts, USA 1938.

EDUCATION Simons received a B.Sc. in Mathematics from MIT in 1958 and, aged 23, a Ph.D. in Mathematics from the University of California, Berkeley.

CAREER After four years as a member of the research staff at the Communications Research Division of the Institute for Defense Analyses he was appointed chairman of the maths department at Stony Brook University. Aged 40 he left academia to run an investment fund that traded in commodities and financial instruments on a discretionary basis. In 1982 he launched the hedge fund Renaissance Technologies. He retired on 1 January 2010, but remains at Renaissance as non-executive chairman.

INVESTMENT PHILOSOPHY Simons is the most successful now living quantitative money manager. Renaissance's models are based on analysing as much data as can be gathered, then looking for non-random movements to make predictions–a strategy that is not easy to copy. The Renaissance approach requires that trades pay off in a limited, specified timeframe. If a big transaction is about to take place on the market Renaissance pushes to the front of the queue. Simons himself explained the strategy in an interview: 'Efficient market theory is correct in that there are no gross inefficiencies but we look at anomalies that may be small in size and brief in time. We make our forecast. Then, shortly thereafter, we re-evaluate the situation and revise our forecast and our portfolio. We do this all day long. We're always in and out and out and in. So we're dependent on activity to make money.' In doing this, Simons surrounds himself with like minds: mathematicians, physicists, astrophysicists, and statisticians. About a third of the 275 employees have doctorates.

OTHER Renaissance Technology manages $15 billion at present and is one of the most profitable hedge funds in the world, despite its high fees. (5 % in fixed fee plus 44 % in performance fee) Simons alone earned an estimated $2.5 billion in 2008, and with an estimated net worth of $10.6 billion, he is one of the richest individuals in the world. The Financial Times named him 'the world's smartest billionaire' 2006. Simons's most influential research involved the discovery and application of certain geometric measurements, and resulted in the Chern–Simons form (also known as Chern–Simons invariants or Chern–Simons theory). Simons has been known to show up at formal business meetings without socks. He is an active participant in a variety of philanthropic endeavours.

Sources: James A. Simons – lecture at International Association of Financial Engineers annual conference 2006; as well as at MIT, 2010; Greenwich Roundtable Medallion Fund; Wikipedia.

LOUIS A.
SIMPSON
USA

ANNUAL YIELD

20%

for **24** YEARS

BENCHMARK 13%

T hink independently. Try to be sceptical of conventional wisdom and to avoid the waves of irrational behaviour and emotion that periodically engulf Wall Street. Such behaviour often leads to excessive prices and, eventually, permanent loss of capital. Don't ignore unpopular companies. On the contrary, such situations often present the greatest opportunities. It is much easier to think independently if you invest for the long term. Short-term developments are often unpredictable and distracting.

Invest in high-return businesses run for the shareholders. In the long run, appreciation in share prices is most directly related to the return the company earns on its shareholders' investment. Try to identify companies that appear able to sustain above-average profitability. Unfortunately, managers who run a profitable business often use excess cash to expand into less profitable endeavours. Be wary of executives with priorities other than maximizing the value of their enterprises for owners.

Pay only a reasonable price, even for an excellent business. Be disciplined in the price you pay for ownership even in a demonstrably superior business. Even the world's greatest business is not a good investment if the price is too high.

BORN Chicago, USA 1937.

EDUCATION Simpson holds a BA from Ohio Wesley University and a Master's degree in Economics from Princeton University in 1960.

CAREER After continuing at Princeton University as an instructor in economics, he started his investment career at Stein Roe and Farnham, where he became a partner. Later he moved to Western Asset Management and took a position as president and CIO. He later held the same positions at the car-insurance company GEICO, which he joined in 1979. After thirty-one years, aged 74, he resigned in 2010, and went on to found a money management firm – SQ Advisors – in Florida together with his wife.

INVESTMENT PHILOSOPHY Simpson is a disciplined stock market value investor. In a recent interview he said that 'My approach is eclectic. I try to read all company documents carefully. We try to talk to competitors. We try to find people more knowledgeable about the business than we are. We do not rely on Wall Street-generated research. We do our own research. We try to meet with top management. We are sort of the polar opposites of a lot of investors. We do a lot of thinking and not a lot of acting. A lot of investors do a lot of acting, and not a lot of thinking.' Despite GEICO being owned by Warren Buffett's investment vehicle, Berkshire Hathaway, the investment profile differs. Simpson invested outside the US and in technology, in contrast to Warren Buffett. He also runs a more concentrated portfolio, where a handful of stocks could represent more than half of the total.

OTHER Despite having managed around $4 billion at GEICO he worked with a small staff – an assistant and an analyst. In an interview he has said that 'The more people you have, the more difficult it is to do well. You have to satisfy everybody. If you have a limited number of decision-makers, they are more likely to agree'. He didn't have a Bloomberg terminal and almost never talked to media. 'So many people broadcast what they buy or sell and it works against them. I'm in favour of people not knowing what we're doing until the last possible moment', he said in one of only two interviews he has given. He remains a director on several public company boards, such as AT&T and Comcast, and in 2006 was named Outstanding Director. In Berkshire Hathaway's annual letter to shareholders in 2004, Warren Buffet devoted one section to Simpson entitled 'Portrait of a Disciplined Investor'.

Sources: Louis A. Simpson; New York Times, April 2007; Berkshire Hathaway; Chicago Tribune, April 2010; Bloomberg; Wikipedia.

JIM
SLATER
UK

BRITAIN'S
FIRST FINANCIAL
GURU

The first key point is to focus on a relatively narrow area and become very expert in it.

The second and most important thing is to cut losses and run profits. Most people do the opposite – they tend to snatch profits and hug losses. In this way inevitably they end up with big losses and small profits instead of the other way around.

The third point is to concentrate on growth shares with forward price earnings ratios less than the future growth rate.

The fourth point is that I am great believer in the importance of cash flow. I always make sure that EPS are exceeded by cash flow on a regular basis. In this way I eliminate potential Enrons.

BORN Chester, UK 1929.

EDUCATION Slater left grammar school at the age of 16 and became a Chartered Accountant when he was 24.

CAREER Slater spent his first nine years after school in industry, culminating in his appointment as deputy sales director of the Leyland Motor Corporation. After successfully writing an investment column under the pseudonym 'Capitalist'—the ghost portfolio of 'Capitalist' appreciated by 68.9 % against the market average of 3.6 % – in 1964 he launched Slater Walker Securities, which collapsed in the wake of the secondary banking crisis of 1973–75. Slater famously found himself to be a 'minus millionaire', owing £1 million more than his assets. Within a few years he repaid all of his debts with interest.

In 1976 he started to invest in property and later in the mining industry as well as biotech and agriculture. In early 1990 he devised a public company statistical guide, Company REFS, for investing based on his investment principles. Since 1975 Slater has been a very active stock market investor and remains so today.

INVESTMENT PHILOSOPHY Slater is a small-cap growth stock market investor. The key figure in his investment approach is the price–earnings growth factor (PEG). A PEG of below one, with earnings growth higher than the multiple, is attractive. His approach is similar to Peter Lynch's, and there is some debate over which of the two devised the PEG. There is, however, no doubt that Slater popularized it in the UK. In addition, Slater demands that a company should show cash flow in excess of earnings and it must have been growing for at least the last three years. Also the company should not be over-geared. His preference for small companies is based on the conviction that 'elephants don't gallop', an expression that he coined. Slater mainly depends for his investments on public data; however, he requires at least three analysts' forecasts before investing. The management's behaviour in terms of their buying shares and being optimistic in their annual reports are also important parts of his approach. Slater has a humble attitude to the market and does not attempt to forecast which way it is going at any point in time. He regards running profits and cutting losses as a key factor in successful investment. His investment style is probably one of the most accessible in the book.

OTHER Despite not managing other people's money, there is a lot of evidence of Slater's investment strategy being successful. His business column and recommendations over the years have proved to be very profitable. A public fund based entirely on his principles would be up 188 % against the market's 73 % in the last three years, and 77 % up over the market's 7 % during the last five years. Slater is first and foremost known in the UK for trying to help the man in the street invest successfully. He has written five investment books as well as thirty books for children. He is still a very active investor and still answers questions about investing on his homepage.

....

Sources: Jim Slater; www.jimslater.org.uk; MFM Slater Growth Fund.

CARLOS SLIM
MEXICO

THE BARGAIN HUNTER

W hen there is a crisis, that's when some are interested in getting out and that's when we are interested in getting in.

I think when you are involved in a business first of all; you need to know the business. After you know the business, you can let the numbers tell you what is happening.

I think one of the big errors people are making right now is thinking that old-style businesses will be obsolete, when actually they will be an important part of this new civilization. Some retail groups are introducing e-commerce and think that the 'bricks' are no longer useful. But they will continue to be important.

BORN Mexico City, Mexico 1940.

EDUCATION He completed his studies in civil engineering at the National Autonomous University of Mexico, where he also taught Algebra and Linear Programming; he taught the latter while still studying, meaning he was simultaneously a student and professor.

CAREER After university, Slim started to work as a stockbroker. In 1965, aged 25, he began to build the foundations of Grupo Carso. Since the 1980s he was a noted businessman in various industrial, real estate, and commercial fields, both through start-ups as well as acquisitions. Slim has now left most of the boards of his companies, and concentrates his efforts on education, health, and employment in Mexico and Latin America.

INVESTMENT PHILOSOPHY Slim could be described as both a contrarian and bargain investor. Two of his most important investments have elements of both. In 1982, during the financial crises in Mexico, companies were sold at less than 10 % of book value. Investors fled Mexico, but Slim bought heavily and it turned out to be very good timing. In the late 1990s he became the largest shareholder in the phone company Telmex when it was privatized. The $1.76 billion value of Telmex has increased by more than twentyfold since privatization. Another example is his recent investment in the failing newspaper industry through his acquisition of almost 10 % of the New York Times. But his investments also have an additional angle—he is searching for virtual monopolies for his companies. Slim is sometimes criticized for ruthlessly driving competitors out of business. His strategy to buy companies cheap and whip them into shape has been consistent over the years. He is said to spot opportunities early and never overpay for anything. Technology is an area of interest, but only in terms of its impact on other industries. He does not use a computer and prefers pen and paper. From being a Latin America investor he is now a global investor. His latest deal was a 28 % stake in the underperforming Dutch telecom operator KPN. Needless to say after the share price had been halved!

OTHER Slim bought his first stocks at the age of twelve, and, as one of six children of a Lebanese immigrant, he was a millionaire by his early twenties. He is now the richest man in the world, with a personal fortune estimated by Forbes in March 2012 to be $69 billion. In all, his companies account for more than one-third of the total value of Mexico's leading stock market index. As one might expect from a successful engineer, Slim is known for being very good with numbers, especially baseball statistics. He has been nicknamed 'the Warren Buffett of Latin America'. In 2007 Slim set aside $4 billion for foundation for health, sports and education. He has a passion for history, art, and nature.

Sources: Carlosslim.com; strategicbusinessteam.com: mycomeup.com; Wikipedia.

DONALD G.
SMITH
USA

ANNUAL YIELD
15.3%
for **30** YEARS
BENCHMARK 8.3%

The universe of investment opportunities is very large and there is a lot of analytical noise in the system. When I started at Capital I realized there were a lot of smart people out there working 12 hours a day analysing every opportunity – how could I possibly beat them? So I said, let's just eliminate 90 per cent of the universe and focus on the lowest price to book decile. To begin with this is a much better pond to fish in. It also gives me a 10 to 1 focus advantage over the competition. We learn much more about these companies than they can learn about the whole universe. Most importantly, when push comes to shove and stock prices are falling, we have an anchor of solid tangible value supporting our stocks, so we can confidently buy at the lows. So I would just say that you need to have a differentiated investment philosophy. After transaction costs, it is a negative-sum game, so not too many people can substantially beat the market over time. You need to have an approach that is unique.

We try to make sure that when we buy something it's so undervalued that natural market forces will cause the stock to go up. We try not to spend a lot of time on anything that is considered active. We might, for example, press management very hard to buy back their own stock instead of doing an acquisition that dilutes book value, but mostly we keep a low profile. Generally managements tend to just listen to you politely and then do what they want to do anyway, unless you have a very large position.

Benjamin Graham said that the opinion people have of management is correlated with the stock price. I have seen dumb managers whose stocks are selling at $10, suddenly become geniuses when their stock goes to $40. One of the attractive things about owning a stock with a low price to book ratio is that it often attracts good management. A good manager at GE for example would rather become the CEO of a company with a stock that's at 80 per cent of book than one in the same industry selling at 1.8x book. We've had companies with average management teams that end up with terrific management, and those companies have become some of our biggest winners.

BORN Not made public.

EDUCATION Smith was awarded a B.Sc. in Finance and Accounting by the University of Illinois, an MBA by Harvard University, and a JD from UCLA Law School.

CAREER Smith began his investment career as an analyst with the Capital Research Company and subsequently worked at the Capital Guardian Trust Co. In 1980, he became the CIO of the Home Insurance Company, and president of Home Portfolio Advisors. Three years later he bought the company and changed the name to Donald Smith & Co. His formal position is CIO.

INVESTMENT PHILOSOPHY Smith is a deep value stock market investor with a special niche. Through extensive research he discovered that the price-book ratio offers the best opportunity to outperform. He and his team only concentrate on the 10 % of stocks with the lowest valuation on tangible assets, and especially the ones selling below their book value. But it is not just screening. He attempts to measure 'tangible' book value using various factors such as adjusting for hidden assets, goodwill, dilution from options and convertible debt, deferred tax, etc. He also requires that target stocks have the prospect of turning the fundamentals positive. That includes talking to the management and industry knowledge in general. The strategy gives you a basket (around 100 positions) with out-of-favour stocks to be kept for three or four years. He always sells when valuation of book value exceeds 200 %.

OTHER He volunteered for Benjamin Graham at UCLA to conduct a study on low P/E strategy. He then realized that earnings were too volatile to base an investment philosophy on, and therefore started playing with book value to develop a better investment approach based on a more stable metric. The average portfolio since inception has had a valuation of tangible book value below one. Donald Smith & Co manages around $4 billion. He has been involved in the Cato Institute, which works to increase the understanding of public policies based on the principles of limited government, free markets, individual liberty, and peace.

Sources: Donald Smith & Co; Graham & Doddsville; Columbia Business School.

GEORGE
SOROS
USA

ANNUAL YIELD

32%

for **31** YEARS

BENCHMARK 11%

I t's not whether you're right or wrong that's important, but how much money you make when you're right and how much you lose when you're wrong.

The prevailing wisdom is that markets are always right. I take the opposite position. I assume that markets are always wrong. I use it as a working hypothesis. It does not follow that one should always go against the prevailing trend. On the contrary, most of the time the trend prevails; only occasionally are the errors corrected. It is only on those occasions that one should go against the trend. This line of reasoning leads me to look for the flaw in every investment thesis. My sense of insecurity is satisfied when I know what the flaw is. It doesn't make me discard the thesis. Rather, I can play it with greater confidence because I know what is wrong with it while market does not

Risk-taking is painful. Either you are willing to bear the pain yourself or you try to pass it on to others. Anyone who is in a risk-taking business but cannot face the consequences is no good. The worse a situation becomes the less it takes to turn it around, the bigger the upside.

BORN Budapest, Hungary 1930.

EDUCATION Soros received a BA in Philosophy at the London School of Economics in 1952.

CAREER Soros started after school at an entry-level position with the London merchant bank Singer & Friedlander. In 1956, Soros moved to New York, where he worked as an arbitrage trader with F. M. Mayer (1956–59) and as an analyst with Wertheim & Co. (1959–63). From 1963 to 1973, he worked at Arnhold and S. Bleichroder, where he attained the position of vice-president. In 1967, he persuaded the company to set up First Eagle, an offshore investment fund for him to run; and, in 1969, it founded the

Double Eagle hedge fund. In 1970 he founded Soros Fund Management, the principal investment advisor to Quantum Fund, a Curaçao-based investment firm. He retired in 2000 but is still the chairman.

INVESTMENT PHILOSOPHY Soros is characterized as a trader and short-term speculator. His deep knowledge of macroeconomic and financial markets in combination with psychology helped him in placing huge bets on the directions of financial markets. He was a master of the top-down analysis of economic trends, often ending up in highly leverage positions in bonds and currencies. One bet in 1992 brought him a profit of more than $1 billion in a single day and the sobriquet 'the man who broke Bank of England'. That said, sometimes things went wrong. When the dot-com bubble burst in 2000, Quantum was not correctly positioned. However, even if his investments are large, and apparently risky, Soros's aim at all times is first and foremost to preserve capital, with yields in second place.

Soros usually moves with the herd and follows the trend, but from time to time seizes the opportunity to break out and take the lead. He relies heavily on his instinct in determining when to act. To sum up his strategy and style, it is very individual and not applicable for the average investor.

OTHER Soros is a superstar among money managers and the king of hedge funds. With his Quantum Fund he had the best performance record of any investment-fund manager in the world in his day. Since it started he has returned over $35 billion in profits to investors, which places Quantum as the second best in the world. Soros has stated that his intention was to earn enough money on Wall Street to support himself as an author and philosopher. Between 1979 and 2011, Soros gave away over $8 billion to human rights, public health, and educational causes. Despite that, he remains one of the fifty wealthiest individuals in the world. He played a significant role in the peaceful transition from communism to capitalism in Hungary (1984–89). He has written thirteen books. His name by birth was Gyögy Schwarz and he changed it temporarily in 1944 to Sándor Kiss to escape the gas chambers.

....

Sources: George Soros, *Soros on Soros: Staying ahead of the curve* (1995); Lois Peitz: *The new investment superstars* (2011); georgesoros.com; Quantum Fund; Wikipedia.

ERIC
SPROTT
CANADA

ANNUAL YIELD
19%
for **14** YEARS
BENCHMARK 6%

→ Earnings per share is the key investment metric. When analysing a company, never forget what the market is willing to pay up for. Earnings growth is critical to any successful equity investment.

→ Be early and take a two to five year horizon. The returns generated by companies in their early stages will grossly outperform those of their later years as they mature. If you're willing to invest early, you can often 'steal' value and dramatically improve your upside potential over time.

→ Small caps always outperform large caps.

BORN Ottawa, Canada 1944.

EDUCATION Sprott received a B.Com. at Carlton University in 1965. He qualified as a Chartered Accountant in 1968.

CAREER Eric began his career as a research analyst at Merrill Lynch in 1972. Aged 37, he branched out on his own to found Sprott Securities, which focused on special situations institutional brokerage. Over the course of the next 20 years, Eric made Sprott Securities into one of Canada's largest independently owned securities firms. Having successfully managed money on the side all those years, Eric decided to found Sprott Asset Management, and subsequently sold his interest in Sprott Securities.

INVESTMENT PHILOSOPHY Sprott's investment approach blends macroeconomic analysis with a fundamental, bottom-up stock-picking style that favours small and mid-cap equities. The cornerstone is a deep knowledge of the metal industry, and more specifically gold and silver. In addition, he has been very successful predicting market trends as well as estimating the big changes in macro, for instance the present finance crises. He takes big bets and has a reputation for running a high-risk strategy. However, his strategy of being long gold and silver and short the stock market has served him well. He has a long-term investing horizon.

OTHER The hedge fund – launched in 2000 – has produced compounded returns of 20 % annually for ten years compared with benchmark of -3 %. He recently launched a Physical Silver Trust in July 2010. The fund returned 68 % in the first four months of opening. Sprott Asset Management manages over $9 billion in assets. Sprott is an active philanthropist and donates to a wide variety of international charities. He is known as Canada's most profiled financial prophet of doom.

Sources: Eric Sprott; Sprott Asset Management; Hedge Funds Review.

MICHAEL
STEINHARDT
USA

ANNUAL YIELD

24%

for **28** YEARS

BENCHMARK 11%

Just as outright euphoria is often a sign of a market top, fear is, for sure, a sign of a market bottom. Time and time again, in every market cycle I have witnessed, the extremes of emotion always appear, even among experienced investors. When the world wants to buy only Treasury Bills, you can almost close your eyes and get long stocks.

The only analytic tool that mattered was an intellectually advantaged disparate view. This included knowing more and perceiving the situation better than others did. It was also critical to have a keen understanding of what the market expectations truly were. Thus, the process by which a disparate perception, when correct, became consensus would almost inevitably lead to meaningful profit.

Beginning at a very early age, I have made cumulatively more judgements, and more investments decisions based on the same kinds of data, than almost anyone else. This process unconsciously leads to a sharpening, a fine-tuning, that, over time, results in fewer mistakes. In this repetitious behaviour, a learning occurs that is not consciously understandable but allows one to develop 'good instincts'. Often listening to an idea led me to an entirely different conclusion to that envisaged by the proponent of that same idea, whose knowledge was far deeper than mine.

BORN New York, USA 1940.

EDUCATION In 1960 Steinhardt graduated from the Wharton School of Finance at the University of Pennsylvania in only three years.

CAREER Steinhardt began his career on Wall Street in research and analyst positions with mutual-fund company Calvin Bullock followed by a similar position at the brokerage firm at Loeb, Rhoades & Co, before founding Steinhardt, Fine, Berkowitz & Co, a hedge fund, in 1967. He retired and closed the fund in 1995. In 2004 he made a comeback through Wisdom Tree, which is the seventh largest index fund in the US based on ETF.

INVESTMENT PHILOSOPHY Even if the fundamentals were the starting-point, he usually ended up being a short-term investor with the normal holding being no longer than a month. 'Our investment style is four yards up the middle in a cloud of dust' as he himself described his investment style with the help of a metaphor from American football. He invested in all forms of assets, but stocks were usually in the majority. In the final years of the fund's existence he also invested abroad, but with dreadful results. In contrast to the other traders in this book, Steinhardt was the opposite of a trend-follower. He preferred to go against the market and short his favourite companies. Neither did he care for technical analysis and graphs. Contrarian is probably the best description of his style, but in large part he was highly individual, and hard to copy. He had no rules or valuation frameworks, but tried simply to think differently. Steinhardt was known for his ability to predict the direction of the stock market. In his time, he was said to have been the most demanding boss on Wall Street.

OTHER He was one of the first prominent hedge-fund managers. No one has been so successful (over 30 % annual gross performance in 28 years) or had that stamina using such an intense investment strategy as Michael Steinhardt. One dollar invested in 1967 in his fund would have grown to $481 in 1995, compared to $19 for S&P 500 in the same period. In 2001 he published his autobiography: *No bull: my life in and out of the markets*. Since retirement he has managed his own money and collected art. He is also a major philanthropist, active in Jewish causes.

....

Sources: Michael Steinhardt, *No bull: my life in and out of markets* (2001); Investopedia; Wikipedia.

J. KRISTOFFER C.
STENSRUD
NORWAY

ANNUAL YIELD

23%

for **19** YEARS

BENCHMARK 11%

Always be very sceptical and pragmatic when investing. You should only invest in companies with business models that are easily understandable. Look at specific companies regardless of what sector they belong to or where they are located, try to use common sense, and have a nose for value. Never buy 'good stories'. Do not rely on information you cannot verify. And remember the first profit-warning is probably not the last.

The market is often wrong. Do your own analysis. Buy when there is a gap between the price and your perceived value of a company. Stay away from rumours and trends. If possible, try to be located away from the financial community; in short think differently. But never be contrarian for contrarianism's own sake – analyse why. Remember, your only weapon is having different expectations and a different time horizon from the other participants in the market who are in the quarterly name-guessing game. Always look at great franchises that for some reason are temporarily discounted. But remember Kodak – franchises may fail.

Invest in equities that are Undervalued, Under-analysed (or wrongly analysed), and Unpopular (or out of fashion) where there are triggers for revaluation. Be paranoid in bull markets and enthusiastic in bear markets.

BORN Trondheim, Norway 1953.

EDUCATION Stensrud obtained an MBA from the Copenhagen Business School in 1979.

CAREER At the age of 25 he co-founded the investment company Borsinformation, where he ended up as portfolio manager in London. He moved back to Norway 1985 to become analyst at Stafonds. After a spell in Denmark as head of research for Carnegie Jensen, he co-founded

Skagen Fondene 1993. His present role is portfolio manager for the largest fund, Skagen Kon-Tiki.

INVESTMENT PHILOSOPHY Stensrud is probably Scandinavia's most successful contrarian investor in the stock market. His sphere of activities is global, and wherever a large and well-run company runs into trouble in the stock market, Skagen's name duly turns up on the list of owners. His favours bottom-up analyses, and sector and nationality are unimportant.

The characteristic target has a strong balance sheet, franchise power, and proven management. The portfolio's average holdings have substantial lower P/E multiples as well as valuation of book value compared to the market. In addition he requires a trigger in the future to unlock the discount in valuation. It does not matter which country the company is located in if the valuation is tempting.

His time horizon is two years and he runs a fairly concentrated portfolio where the ten biggest positions account for about half of it. He seldom travels and works on the basis that the consensus is always wrong.

OTHER Skagen Kon-Tiki, which Stensrud manages at present, is the best-performing emerging markets fund. In the last ten years it has delivered 18.5 % annually, compared with benchmark of 9.5 %.

Assets under management in Skagen Fondene total around $15 billion, and the fund operates out of the small town of Stavanger in Norway, far away from any financial centre. Stensrud counts Mikael Randel (p. 170) and Anthony Bolton (p. 58) as his mentors, and prefers to work in the summer when other investors are on holiday. He is interested in meteorology and sports a ponytail.

....

Sources: Kristoffer Stensrud; Skagen fonder; Skagen Vekst; Skagen Global; Skagen Kon-Tiki.

LÁSZLÓ
SZOMBATFALVY
SWEDEN

THE MOST PROMINENT AND SUCCESSFUL INVESTOR IN SWEDEN

Adjust your required rate of return to the share's specific level of risk. Do not rely on risk measured as volatility. The real risk is found in:

(i) External risks: Earnings forecasts, competitive environment, currencies, the sector's risk profile, and pricing power.

(ii) Internal risks: Financial risk (always check the equity ratio, margin after paid interest and adjust for goodwill), growth strategy (acquisitions increase the risk), and management.

Try to understand the risk level by projecting a most optimistic and a most pessimistic long-term scenario. The actual outcome will with a fairly high probability – but not a certainty – be between your two extremes. The range between these extreme forecasts becomes the measure of risk. Depending on the risk, the required rate of return should be 5–15 percentage points above the long bond rate.

Be selective. You do not need to be fully invested over time. Just keep the bargains. Do not wait to sell overvalued stock due to lack of substitutes or to avoid tax. Regard the capital gains tax as a mark of success.

Never put more at stake than you can afford to lose. Both unpredictable and predictable (but not predicted) events can trigger a general fall in stock markets. Never confuse the unlikely with the impossible.

BORN Budapest, Hungary 1927.

EDUCATION After three years studying law at university he left without a degree when the communist regime began to control the university courses. Being one of few occupations not politicized in Hungary, he took a state artist academy degree in his hobby and became a magician. He fled to Sweden in 1956, where he attended trade school and took a correspondence course in business while working.

CAREER In Sweden Szombatfalvy began by working as a magician. Next he worked twelve years in Shell's finance department. In 1966 he began to invent valuation models for stocks. Five years later he was already successful in his investments and then left Shell. He became partner in Alfred Berg (a local brokerage firm), but his efforts were concentrated on his own portfolio. He left the capital market just before the crash in 1987 and retired.

INVESTMENT PHILOSOPHY Szombatfalvy worked according to a valuation model he had developed, not too different from the famous 'Gordon model'. He focused on risk, discounted dividends, adjusted earnings, and adjusted capital. Return on adjusted equity was perhaps the single most important figure. He always took a long-term view and never invested in companies with a short history. In his model he also assumed that extremely high profitability was going to end sooner or later. Companies with growing capacity for dividend in connection with low dividend at present became his favourite targets.

OTHER Due to Szombatfalvy's cooperation with the Swedish business magazine Affärsvärlden he has educated and influenced most of Sweden's investors and analysts. Starting from nothing, (he borrowed $1,000) he has become one of the wealthiest individuals in Sweden only by stock picking. If we assume that he instead started with $1,000 in equity he has annually performed more than 30% for 46 years. He has become one of the wealthiest individuals in Sweden. He has recently written two books, in one of which, *The Greatest Challenges of Our Time*, he uses his knowledge of risk to warn of the risks mankind is taking with the environment and that the present political system is not capable of handling the situation. The book has been translated into five languages. Last year he founded The Global Challenge Foundation – with the goal of creating better conditions and effective actions against the global threat to mankind.

....

Sources: László Szombatfalvy.

ANTON
TAGLIAFERRO
AUSTRALIA

ANNUAL YIELD

11.2%

for **14** YEARS

BENCHMARK 8.4%

The media and stockbrokers always seem totally focused on the levels and the fluctuations of companies' share prices or infatuated with the latest fad. As an investor one should focus solely on the underlying valuation and sustainable income streams that a company generates.

If you don't fully trust the motives or integrity of a company's management, never buy the shares – there are plenty of other honest, hardworking, and focused management teams out there.

When investing, always question your own assumptions, and never be complacent or arrogant. If you ever start to think you are bigger or better than the sharemarket, it has a habit of always turning around and kicking you in the bum!

BORN Malta 1959.

EDUCATION Tagliaferro obtained a BA in accountancy at City University in London, 1981. Three years later he qualified as a Chartered Accountant.

CAREER Tagliaferro began his career at the accounting firm Deloitte's in London in 1981. After five years he left accountancy to work as a portfolio manager at Perpetual Funds Management. At the age of 39, after a few years first with County NatWest and then BNP, Tagliaferro founded Investors Mutual Limited (IML), an equities-fund manager based in Australia that specializes in the Australian stock market.

INVESTMENT PHILOSOPHY Tagliaferro is a conservative value investor with the stock market as his chosen field. He mainly focuses on quality companies with strong competitive edges that generate stable and predictable revenue streams. The companies must also have strong balance sheets and dependable management. He frequently chooses to invest in companies that are currently unpopular. Overall, the shares in his portfolio have a lower-risk profile and higher yield than the market as a whole.

OTHER Tagliaferro is probably the Italian football club AC Milan's most fervent Australian supporter, and is a local sponsor of the AC Milan football academy in Sydney. In addition, he has founded a charitable foundation and is involved in several relief organizations in Australia.

Sources: Anton Tagliaferro; IML.

SIR JOHN M.
TEMPLETON
USA/UK

ANNUAL YIELD
14.5%
for **38** YEARS
BENCHMARK 8%

Remain flexible and open-minded about every type of investment. There are times to buy blue-chip stocks, cyclical stocks, corporate bonds convertibles bond, US Treasury investments, and so on. And there are times to sit on cash, because sometimes cash enables you to take advantage of investment opportunities. The fact is there is no one kind of investment that is always best.

Diversify. In stocks and bonds, as in much else, there is safety in numbers. So you must diversify, by company, by industry, by risk, and by country. Having said that, I should note that, for most of the time, most of our clients' money has been in common stocks.

Ethics and spiritual principles should be the basis of everything we do in life. All that we say, all that we think. Every activity should be based on that, including selection of investments. You wouldn't want to be an owner of a company that is producing harm for the public, and therefore you wouldn't want to be the owner of a share in a company that's producing harm to the public. We should all give great attention to that, and probably it will be profitable to you, because companies that are harmful ordinarily do not prosper for very long. You will be better off with companies that are truly beneficial. They will go up more in price and grow more rapidly.

BORN Tennessee, USA 1912. Died in the Bahamas, 2008.

EDUCATION Sir John graduated in 1934 from Yale University. He financed a portion of his tuition by playing poker, a game at which he excelled. He attended Oxford University as a Rhodes Scholar and earned an MA in law in 1936.

CAREER In 1937 he co-founded an investment firm that would become Templeton, Dobbrow & Vance. In 1954, Templeton also started the Templeton Growth Fund, based in Nassau in the Bahamas. Over the next twenty-five years, Templeton created some of the world's largest and most successful international investment funds. He sold his Templeton funds in 1992 to the Franklin Group.

INVESTMENT PHILOSOPHY One of the twentieth century's top contrarians. The best description is probably value-contrarian investor. His investing style can be summed up as looking for value investments, what he called 'bargain hunting' in a 'search for companies around the world that offered low prices and an excellent long-term outlook.' The more countries you visited the better was his maxim They had to be quality stocks and he held onto them for six or seven years.

Sir John believed that the best bargains were in stocks that were completely neglected—those that other investors were not even studying. He preferred to communicate with businessmen instead of Wall Street. He had no faith in technical analysis, but focussed entirely on fundamentals. The economists of the Austrian School were his intellectual ideals, and he did not invest in countries that he regarded as being too socialist.

Sir John attributed much of his success to his ability to remain cheerful, avoid anxiety, and stay disciplined. He became known for 'avoiding the herd'. He was a student of Benjamin Graham, and one of his abiding legacies was the importance of diversified portfolios.

OTHER Templeton became a billionaire by pioneering the use of globally diversified mutual funds. Before then, investing overseas was absolutely unheard of. His Templeton Growth, Ltd. (an investment fund), established in 1954, was among the first to invest in Japan in the mid-1960s. Money Magazine called him 'arguably the greatest global stock picker of the century.' Uninterested in consumerism, he drove his own car, never flew first class and lived year-round in the Bahamas. Sir John became an active philanthropist worldwide through his John Templeton Foundation, which supports spiritual and scientific research. A lifelong Presbyterian, he most of all went long on God. Every annual meeting in the fund began with a prayer. He financed his studies at school by playing poker.

Sources: Gary Moore, *Ten Golden Rules For Financial Success – Riches I've Gathered from Legendary Mutual Fund Manager Sir John M. Templeton* (1996); Investopedia; Wikipedia

DAVID
TEPPER
USA

ANNUAL YIELD
31%
for **17** YEARS
BENCHMARK 6%

→ Sometimes the hardest thing to do is to do nothing.

→ We are a herd leader. We are in front of the pack. We are one of the first movers. First movers are interesting. You get the good grass first.

→ Over time, I think you just treat people right, run your business right, your life right—it's the whole package.

BORN Pittsburgh, USA 1957.

EDUCATION Tepper obtained his M.Sc. in Industrial Administration from Carnegie Mellon Business School (now the Tepper School of Business) in 1982.

CAREER After completing high school he entered the finance industry, working for Equibank as a credit analyst in the Treasury department. After his MBA, Tepper accepted a position in the Treasury department of Republic Steel in Ohio. In 1984, he was recruited to Keystone Mutual Funds (now part of Evergreen Funds) in Boston, and in 1985 moved to Goldman Sachs, where he worked for eight years. His primary focus was bankruptcies and special situations. He left Goldman in December 1992 and started Appaloosa Management in early 1993.

INVESTMENT PHILOSOPHY Tepper is categorized as a distressed-debt investor, but he really analyses and invests in the entire capital structure of distressed companies, from senior secured debt to sub-debt and post-bankruptcy equity. High-yield bonds and distressed securities are the cornerstone in the fund. He has a contrarian investment style with concentrated bets, and he tries to be invested at the turning point, which is the most difficult strategy. That sometimes brings a volatile performance: down 25 % in 2008 but up 133 % in 2009. He invests in all asset classes with no geographical limitations, but normally does not use leverage. He brings the macro perspective to the micro perspective. Despite being a trader at Goldman Sachs his investment approach is fundamental.

OTHER Appaloosa Management manages over $12 billion from a small town in New Jersey. In 2009 he earned $4 billion and, according to him, he personally has made around 40 % annually since it was started in 1993. Forbes estimated his wealth to $5.5 billion in 2012. Maybe his most famous deals were to buy into distressed debt and securities in Enron and Worldcom after they defaulted. His inspiration came from his father who was an accountant and active in the stock market. Tepper therefore started early and traded in the market even when at university. His first investment, Pennsylvania Engineering Company Co. went into bankruptcy, however. He is very interested in baseball, and is co-owner of the Pittsburgh Pirates.

Sources: CNBC; New York Times; Bloomberg; lecture at the Tepper School of Business;Wall Street Oasis; Appaloosa Hedge Fund; Wikipedia.

EDWARD O.
THORP
USA

ANNUAL YIELD
20%
for **28** YEARS
BENCHMARK 11%

→ Think for yourself: check the facts and form your own opinions.
→ Do what you love and the money will follow.
→ Life is a journey: it's what you do along the way that matters.

BORN Chicago, USA 1932.

EDUCATION Next to Simons, Thorp is probably the academic heavyweight in this book. He studied at UCLA, where he took a BA and MA in Physics, and a Ph.D. in Mathematics in 1958.

CAREER Thorp never really left academe. He started by working at the famous university MIT for a couple of years, and was then a professor of mathematics at New Mexico State University. He then returned to his alma mater where he spent 17 years as a professor of mathematics and finance. Thorp's first hedge fund was Princeton-Newport Partners, which he started 1969. At the age of 57, he founded the hedge fund Edward O. Thorp & Associated where he still is the president. Even though he officially retired in 2002, he continues trading and undertaking his academic work.

INVESTMENT PHILOSOPHY Thorp is a quantitative trader who relies wholly on sophisticated mathematical techniques and computer models to identify arbitrage all over the market. In the beginning Thorp mainly focused on warrants, convertibles, or derivatives trading out of sync with the underlying stocks. Parallel with this, he worked for eight years to create a computer model to rank stocks from best to worse. All was based on statistical analyses and hedge funds were always neutral. Thorp does not analyse specific stocks or read brokerage research. He has said that he 'laughs at the idea that anyone could know enough about all the publicly traded stocks to suss out the ones with long-term appeal'. But he has also said 'You can always do as well as the average player by picking stocks at random and holding them a long time'.

His is a trading-oriented environment with roughly 3,000 transactions a day. In contrast to most hedge funds, Thorp prefers to operate with small assets under management, keeping the fund at about $300 million by closing it often and distributing profits regularly. Thorp has a flexible approach to investing, has continuously come up with new models, and looks worldwide for opportunities. For a while he concentrated on Japanese warrants where he made a fortune.

OTHER Taking into account the very low risk, Thorp's performance is amazing. His first hedge fund did not have a losing quarter in 19 years. The weakest year was 8 % plus in 1973. He was one of the first investors to capitalize on discrepancies between futures and stock prices. He was also the first to use computers to program arbitrage, before the techniques became widely adopted. In addition he also invented the first portable computer in 1961. Thorp has written five books, of which *Beat the Dealer* became a best seller. It presented the first scientific system ever devised to break a major casino, including how to beat the bank at Black Jack by counting cards. After being 'too' successful he was banned from all Las Vegas casinos. He is an accomplished amateur photographer, astronomer, and runner, and he has never bought a lottery ticket.

Sources: Edward Thorp; edwardothorp.com; Ken Kurson, "Having the edge on the market" (2003).

PAUL
TUDOR JONES
USA

ANNUAL YIELD
21%
for **25** YEARS
BENCHMARK 8.5%

→ The most important rule of trading is to play great defence, not great offence. Every day I assume every position I have is wrong. I know where my stop risk points are going to be. I do that so I can define my maximum possible draw down. Hopefully, I spend the rest of the day enjoying positions that are going in my direction. If they are going against me, then I have a game plan for getting out.

→ I believe the very best money is made at the market turns. Everyone says you get killed trying to pick tops and bottoms, and you make all your money by playing the trend in the middle. Well for twelve years I have been missing the meat in the middle, but I have made a lot of money at tops and bottoms.

→ You adapt, evolve, compete, or die.

BORN Memphis, USA 1954.

EDUCATION Tudor Jones earned an undergraduate degree in Economics in 1976 at the University of Virginia. He dropped out of Harvard Business School.

CAREER Tudor Jones started as a clerk on the trading floors and then became a broker for E. F. Hutton. After going it on his own for a couple of years he was hired to trade cotton futures at the New York Cotton Exchange. Aged 26 he founded Tudor Investment Corporation, now the Tudor Group, where he still serves as president.

INVESTMENT PHILOSOPHY He is a self-made trader and hedge fund manager with a broad and diverse allocation of capital wherever opportunities may emerge around the world. About half of Jones's trading depends on technical analysis using historical price charts to predict market moves. He operates in most of the assets classes, even venture capital. The bulk of the investments are macro trades, which in the past represented a bit above half of the assets, and trades in global equities accounted for roughly one-third. This is how he describes his own style: 'I'd say that my investment philosophy is that I don't take a lot of risk; I look for opportunities with tremendously skewed reward–risk opportunities. Don't ever let them get into your pocket – that means there's no reason to leverage substantially. There's no reason to take substantial amounts of financial risk ever, because you should always be able to find something where you can skew the reward risk relationship so greatly in your favour that you can take a variety of small investments with great reward risk opportunities that should give you minimum draw down pain and maximum upside opportunities.'

OTHER The quotes from a video in 1987 with Tudor Jones say a lot about his work profile: 'To do the job right requires such an enormous amount of concentration. It's physically and emotionally mandatory that you find some time to relax. And you've got to be able to turn it off like that. There will be times though that I get so incredibly excited about a trade or even a project that I'll wake up at 4 o'clock in the morning and there's no way in hell that I'm going back to sleep. I'll sit there in my dreams and trade for four hours.' Tudor Jones manages around $11 billion at present through different investments partnership. He is famous for predicting the 1987 stock market crash, a year when he performed around 200 %. As of September 2011, he was estimated to have a net worth of $3.2 billion. In 1976 he earned a welterweight boxing championship. Jones is the founder of the Robin Hood Foundation, a philanthropic organization dedicated to fighting poverty in New York City, mainly backed by hedge-fund operators.

Sources: Paul Tudor Jones; Bloomberg; Jack D. Schwager, *Market Wizards* (1988); chinese-school.netfirms.com/; Hedge Funds Review 2004; Trader: the documentary – with Paul Tudor Jones 1987); Wikipedia.

ARNOLD
VAN DEN BERG
USA

ANNUAL YIELD
14.2%
for **38** YEARS
BENCHMARK 11.7%

Over the past 75 years, we have had 13 recessions, periods of high inflation, multiple wars (including a world war), oil shocks, and real estate bubbles. While most of these events caused sell-offs in the market in the short run, they were not the factors that influenced stock prices in the long run. In fact, many of these events created buying opportunities for long-term investors. Contrary to the mainstream media, and irrespective of people's opinions, there are only three major factors that influence stock prices in the long run: company fundamentals, inflation, and interest rates. Period!

There are four basic rules investors should follow: (1) Buy stocks only when they are selling at significant discounts to their intrinsic values. Depending on the size and quality of the company, a discount of 50 per cent to 70 per cent typically puts the odds on a successful return in your favour. (2) Sell stocks when they are approaching 80 per cent of their intrinsic values, as the reward-to-risk ratios are generally no longer in your favour. (3) Ignore the 'wisdom' and advice given from Wall Street's economic projections and government pronouncements. Disregard media hype and sensationalism. (4) If you find there is nothing cheap to buy, be patient, and wait in cash or cash equivalent holdings until you can find stocks selling at bargain level prices. This will help you avoid a permanent loss of capital.

Buying a great company does not guarantee you have made a great investment. I cannot emphasize this enough. People ask me all the time, 'What do you think about this company or that company?' They continue with, 'It's a wonderful company with a great product, great management, and great marketing.' Everything may be wonderful – but it has been my experience that this is not where you make your money. A great company is not a great investment unless you buy it at a great price. No matter what you buy, there is point where you can pay too much and it diminishes the value. So the fact that a company is a great company is only part of the equation. The most important thing to remember is that the price you pay for a company will ultimately determine your return.

BORN Amsterdam, the Netherlands 1939.

EDUCATION High school. Received his securities licence in 1968.

CAREER Arnold Van Den Berg began his investment career selling mutual funds for John Hancock Insurance, and later for Capital Securities. Founded Century Management in 1974. He founded Century Management at the age of 35, and he still acts as CEO and oversees its investments.

INVESTMENT PHILOSOPHY Van Den Berg is one of the most experienced value investors in today's stock market. He has used the same valuation methods for 38 years. He applies value investment strategies as his investment philosophy. His investment research is aimed at determining a company's appraised value, often referred to as its intrinsic value. Investments are then made at a significant discount, normally 40 % to 65 % below the company's current intrinsic value – his chosen safety margin. Van Den Berg usually holds 35–40 companies when fully invested, and invests primarily in companies based in the US. From time to time, cash forms a substantial part of the portfolio. He considers himself a disciple of Benjamin Graham.

OTHER Van Den Berg has the third longest track record of the 99 investors. He made his decisions regarding investment philosophy by studying the big stock market decline between 1968 and 1974. He concluded that the managers who used a value-based investment strategy both protected their clients' capital better and provided more consistent investment results than managers using other investment strategies. He is a holocaust survivor and has started a foundation called Children Blessing Children.

Sources: Arnold Van Den Berg; Century Management; All-Cap Value.

BJÖRN
WAHLROOS
FINLAND

THE MOST SUCCESSFUL INVESTOR IN FINLAND

B eing an economist by training and for-mer profession, I tend to think markets are mostly quite efficient, offering the seasoned investor little more than the market return corresponding to the level of risk he is willing to bear. Every once in a while, however—maybe every three to five years or so – 'panics' or euphorias tend to materialize. Identifying them and the asset mispricing they cause is the sole cause for 'supernormal' returns I have ever found in the least bit credible.

BORN Helsinki, Finland 1952.

EDUCATION Wahlroos graduated in 1975 with an M.Sc. at the Hanken School of Economics in Helsinki and got his D.Sc. in Economics in 1979.

CAREER Aged 33, having been a professor at the Hanken School of Economics in Finland as well as visiting professor at Brown University and the Kellogg School of Management at Northwestern University in the US, he switched careers by joining the Union Bank of Finland (UBF) as vice-president. Three years later he was appointed executive vice-president and head of Investment Banking & Treasury at UBF. Together with half a dozen colleagues, Wahlroos bought out the investment banking operations of UBF in 1992. In 2000 Wahlroos merged his banking group into Sampo-Leonia and took over as president and CEO of the combined company. He still serves as chairman of Sampo, and remains its largest individual shareholder.

INVESTMENT PHILOSOPHY Wahlroos's investments have so far been limited to financial assets in northern Europe, something he, together with Sampo's management, has done very well. Selling assets at the top and buying assets cheap has been his winning mantra. He has built up the present company (Sampo), much like Warren Buffett and Preem Watsa, based on insurance, but it is not managing the money in bonds or equity that justifies his record – it is the timing of selling and buying companies in the stock market or outside it. It is a contrarian approach, which requires confidence in macro as well as courage.

OTHER For the last eight years the average yearly performance (NAV per share) at Sampo has been above 15 % (benchmark 9 %). He is one of the richest individuals in Finland and chairman in several blue-chip companies. While a student, Wahlroos was involved in left-wing politics.

Sources: Björn Wahlroos; Sampo; Wikipedia.

RALPH
WANGER
USA

ANNUAL YIELD
16%
for **33** YEARS
BENCHMARK 12%

You have to be very careful about the fad in the market. It is pushed by the brokers and is usually wrong. Every bad idea starts as a good idea. It is like the first glass of champagne. Too much of a good thing gets bad. Try to avoid these things.

I always have a long-term holding in connection with low turnover and it is useful to invest in themes. That is the way to differ from the crowd. Because if you invest like everybody else, you will perform like everybody else. But it is not easy. Long term means a five year outlook, and that is very much guesswork. Therefore it is good to rely on themes, but they must be broad ideas.

Since the Industrial Revolution began, heading downstream – investing in businesses that will benefit from new technology rather than investing in the technology companies themselves – has often been the smarter strategy. Even some of the best technology companies, like for example Digital Equipment, failed.

BORN Chicago, USA 1934.

EDUCATION Wanger received his BA and MA from MIT, graduating in 1955. He is a CFA.

CAREER He started out in the insurance business and then began his investing career with Harris Associates in Chicago in 1960. He worked as a securities analyst and has been the portfolio manager of Acorn Fund since its was started in 1970. He founded Wanger Asset Management in 1992, aged 58, after resigning from Harris Associates and taking the Acorn Fund with him. He stepped down from day-to-day duties in 2005, but still serves on several boards and writes quarterly letters as a senior advisor.

INVESTMENT PHILOSOPHY Wanger is a small-cap growth stock market investor. He looks for smaller companies with financial strength, high market share, good customer services, and entrepreneurial managers. The businesses should also be understandable and have a growth potential. While these criteria could seem common, Wanger puts strict limits on the valuation: it must be reasonably priced in connection to earnings and cash flow. That approach saved him from joining the dot-com bubble. He demands that the investment be based on a theme; strong economic, social, and technological trends – it doesn't matter which as long as they are successful and can increase sales and profit for several years. These also drive corporate sales and profits. He requires a long-term trend in order to have the stamina to hold stocks with a five-year, or sometimes ten-year, investment horizon. The focus on small cap is based on the conviction that the smaller companies in general are overlooked by Wall Street. As he said himself, another reason is that 'Chances are things have changed enough so that whatever made you a success thirty years ago doesn't work anymore. I think that by concentrating on smaller companies, you improve your chances of catching the next wave.' He usually avoids turnarounds, start-ups, and new issues, which tend to be weakly financed. He does not put a lot of emphasis on spotting the market direction, or as he is quoted saying: 'If you believe you or anyone else has a system that can predict the future of the stock market, the joke is on you.' Most of the performance in Acorn Fund comes from many unglamorous small companies.

OTHER Given that Wanger manages almost $20 billion (up from $8 million at the start) in the Acorn Fund, his performance even more impressive. In a national survey by US Today, professional money managers voted for the investment professional whom they would most like to manage their money –Wanger was top of the list. He was the first manager to receive the prestigious Morningstar's Fund Manager Lifetime Achievement Award, which recognizes mutual-fund managers who throughout their careers have delivered outstanding long-term performance. His book *Zebra In Lion Country* turns on the analogy of well-dressed fund managers as zebras; some of them will be taken by the lions.

Sources: Ralph Wanger; Ralph Wanger and Everett Mattlin, *Zebra in Lion Country: Ralph Wanger's Guide to Investment Survival* (1999); Wanger Asset Management; Acorn Fund Investopedia.

PREM
WATSA
CANADA

ANNUAL YIELD
23.5%
for **26** YEARS
BENCHMARK 8%

The market is manic-depressive. Sometimes it buys at a high price and sells at a low price. Don't ever think that it knows more than you.

People have a difficult time taking the long-term view. Human nature hasn't changed, and people want to do well in the short term and make money as fast as possible. They can't handle fluctuations. So if people buy something at $10 and it goes to $7 or $8 or $5, they think they have made a mistake and they want to sell. They can't look through that to the long term, which, of course, was Benjamin Graham's great contribution.

We try to be careful about whom we become partners with, who we associate ourselves with. We have this fair and friendly culture that we've talked about. This fair and friendly culture is one of our guiding principles, we want partners who fit with that, who think long term. We're not trying to make money at the expense of everything else. If they don't buy into our values, we don't want to be partners with them, so that helps in terms of spreading our culture to any company we acquire.

BORN Hyderabad, India 1950.

EDUCATION Watsa graduated from the Indian Institute of Technology with a degree in Chemical Engineering in 1971. The next year he moved to Canada and got an MBA from the Richard Ivey School of Business of the University of Western Ontario.

CAREER He started in the insurance business by working ten years for the Confederation Life Insurance Co. at the investment wing in Toronto. After one year at the start-up GW Asset Management, Watsa, aged 34, co-founded Hamblin. The next year Hamblin took control of Markel Financial Holdings, which later was renamed Fairfax (short for 'fair and friendly acquisitions'). He still serves as president and chief executive of Fairfax Financial Holdings.

INVESTMENT PHILOSOPHY Watsa is a value investor and a disciple of Benjamin Graham, looking for buying a dollar for 50 cents. The portfolio, now over $20 billion, is invested mainly in stocks and bonds worldwide, wherever value can be found. He is known for going against the grain and spending lots of time making a case against conventional wisdom. Despite his aim to search for a margin of safety he sometimes ends up investing in troublesome technology companies (Research In Motion) and banks (Bank of Ireland) and Greek bonds. He has also successfully invested in credit default swaps in 2008. He describes his investment philosophy thus: 'We are buying with the idea that the stocks we buy could go down in the short-term and that is not going to affect us. You have to be able to buy with cash and not go on margin or borrow money to buy stocks'. In addition to the bottom-up valuation, Watsa takes a top-down approach to the macroeconomics. He runs a fairly concentrated portfolio of some fifty positions, and acts like a hedge fund by hedging assets from time to time.

OTHER He has an uncanny gift of predicting financial crises and predicted the crash of 1987, the Japanese collapse of 1990 and the financial meltdown of 2008. He is said to have named his son Ben after Benjamin Graham. Sir John Templeton was a close friend and mentor. Like Buffett, Watsa based his fortune on a bedrock of insurance. He has been called the 'Canadian Warren Buffett'. Fairfax was Canada's most profitable corporation in 2008, and according to Toronto Life, Watsa's personal wealth is above $4 billion. Fairfax Holdings invests at least 1 % of its pre-tax profits every year in the communities where the company operates.

Sources: Prem Watsa; Toronto Life, CFA Magazine, September 2011; Toronto Life April 2009; GuruFocus 27 September 2011; Fairfax Holding; BestCashCow.com; Wikipedia.

WALLY
WEITZ
USA

ANNUAL YIELD
13%
for **28** YEARS
BENCHMARK 10%

Mutual-fund investors consistently snatch defeat from the jaws of victory. Dozens of studies show (approximately) the same results: stocks have earned about 10 per cent per year over many decades; stock mutual funds have earned about 9 per cent per year (the difference being expenses); stock mutual-fund investors have earned about 3 per cent per year. The reason for this 6 per cent shortfall is that fund investors regularly sell the loser of the previous period and buy the winner of the previous period. Fund investors cost themselves 6 per cent per year by chasing performance. Don't do it.

Measure value of business, then buy low and sell high. The value of a business is (roughly) measurable and usually changes gradually. The company's stock price may fluctuate over a wide range, giving the investor the opportunity to buy at a bargain price and sell at a full or premium price. This approach requires patience, dis-cipline, and the courage of one's convictions, but it dramatically improves the investor's odds of success.

Turn off CNBC and turn on the History Channel. The day-to-day news and opinion served up by the financial media tends to foster short-term thinking and emotional behaviour. It can be quite counter-productive to good, long-term investing. Understanding the factors that affect a company's ability to generate cash for its owners over a period of many years is much more important.

Management matters. Every few years, most companies are faced with a big deci-sion – a problem to deal with, an oppor-tunity to make a bold, positive move, or a chance to make or avoid a big mistake. We want to feel confident that management will be honest with itself, understand the risks involved, think of shareholders as part-ners, and pursue the long-term, per share, value of the business.

BORN Newton, Massachusetts, USA 1944

EDUCATION Weitz earned a BA in Economics at Carleton College and is a CFA charterholder.

CAREER He started as a small-cap analyst at G. A. Saxton. After three years he joined Chiles, Heider & Co., Inc., a regional brokerage firm in Omaha, where he spent ten years as an analyst and portfolio manager. Aged 39 he founded Wallace R. Weitz & Company where he is president and portfolio manager.

INVESTMENT PHILOSOPHY Weitz is a long-term stock market value investor. His investment style combines Graham's price sensitivity and insistence on a 'margin of safety' with a conviction that qualitative factors that allow companies to have some control over their own destinies can be more important than statistical measurements, such as historical book value or reported earnings. In his own words, he searches 'for securities with growth and well-managed businesses of any size which have honest, competent management and then estimate the price that an informed, rational buyer would pay for 100 % of the business'. It has to be a company whose business he understands. Weitz likes firms that offer services rather than those that make a tangible product. He feels that service firms are less vulnerable to pricing pressure and are therefore in greater control of their own destinies. He also likes companies that generate plenty of free cash flow. When he can't find stocks that meet his exacting value criteria, Weitz simply increases his cash holdings and waits at the sideline.

OTHER Weitz's investment career began aged twelve, when he invested his profits from various entrepreneurial ventures. He now manages approximately $4 billion. When he's not playing bridge with Warren Buffett he enjoys golf, skiing, tennis, reading, and working with charitable and educational foundations.

Sources: Wally Weitz; Wally Weitz Funds; Partners III Opportunity Fund; Forbes.

MARTIN J.
WHITMAN
USA

ANNUAL YIELD
11.7%
for **22** YEARS

BENCHMARK 6.5%

→ It's wrong to obsess about the income statement and to ignore the balance sheet. It's wrong to value a business solely on the basis of what it might earn in the future to the exclusion of what it owns in the present. It's wrong to demand more of financial statements prepared in accordance with generally accepted accounting principles than they can deliver. What these financial documents offer is not the truth, but a set of objective benchmarks with which an intelligent investor can arrive at a useful semblance of the truth.

→ We think diversification is only a surrogate, and usually a poor surrogate, for knowledge, control, and price consciousness.

→ With stocks you have to worry about the market, with debt I just have to understand the contract. If my analysis is right, I'll make money.

BORN New York, USA 1925.

EDUCATION Whitman graduated in business administration from Syracuse University in 1949 (which renamed its School of Management after Whitman following a large donation). He holds a Master's in Economics from the New School for Social Research and is an adjunct faculty member at Yale School of Management.

CAREER After university, Whitman worked for a string of investment firms in New York City and Philadelphia. He began his career as a security analyst at Shearson Hammill before working for the Rosenwald family, of Sears Roebuck fortune. Aged 49 he ventured out on his own and founded M. J. Whitman LLC, a full-service broker–dealer. He established himself as an investment banker, expert witness in shareholder litigations, and turnaround specialist for bankrupt companies. He also managed an open-end investment company, Equity Strategies. Aged 65 he founded Third Avenue Management; he is still portfolio manager there, as well as chairman of the board and co-chief investment officer.

INVESTMENT PHILOSOPHY Whitman is a long-term bottom-up stock market value investor who depends on fundamental analysis. He has an opportunistic approach and is not constrained by market capitalization, industry sector, or geographic location. His investment mantra is 'safe and cheap'. The focus is on analysing the current balance sheet of companies that he and his team believe have the potential to create value in the long term, withstanding cyclical downturns and evolving as leaders among their competition. Six main criteria are crucial: strong finances; high-quality assets with conservative and appropriate leverage; competent management; a proven track record and interests aligned with outside, passive, minority shareholders; an understandable business; a comprehensible business model with meaningful financial information readily available. A sound political and regulatory environment means the presence of a legal framework that protects a business and shareholder rights. A significant discount to intrinsic value means that it is priced substantially below a conservative estimate of the business' value as a private entity or takeover candidate. Attractive growth prospects means the potential for attractive growth in the value of a company's net assets over the next five years.

He regards macro data such as interest rates, private consumption, etc. as unimportant for investors as long as the political system is stable. The portfolio normally consists of roughly 100 positions and has a low turnover. Whitman will not invest unless one of the larger accountant companies has done the auditing. Whitman does not believe in market efficiency because the army of analysts and portfolio managers focus on the wrong things: the income statement and future earnings.

OTHER Whitman is a strong opponent of the direction of recent changes in generally accepted accounting principles (GAAP) in US. He is a frequent speaker and commentator on the financial services community, criticizing, for example, the free market in the sense advocated by Milton Friedman and Friedrich Hayek. Whitman's view is that in well-run industrial economies, there is a marriage between government and the private sector, each benefiting from the other. He has written three books. Third Avenue Management manages more than $20 billion of assets. He has taught at the Yale School of Management for over thirty years. He served in the Navy during the Second World War.

Sources: Martin J. Whitman & Martin Shubik, *The Aggressive Conservative Investor* (2005); Martin J. Whitman; The first quarterly letter from Third Avenue Funds"; MSCI World Index; Forbes; Wikipedia.

ROBERT W.
WILSON
USA

ANNUAL YIELD
30%
for **37** YEARS
BENCHMARK 7%

Never stay completely out of the market due to lack of major opportunities. There are always major opportunities.

The ability to take pain, because one is wrong so much of the time, is the most important characteristic of a star. It's amazing how few can do it. I remember having lunch with a friend who is, really, much smarter than I am – we both agree on that – and who asked me why I made so much more money than he did. I told him that I could be down 40 per cent from time to time and live with myself. He admitted he couldn't.

It's important to thoroughly understand WHY whatever market you are playing – stocks, bonds, or whatever – is behaving the way it is. A huge amount of intellectual input influences prices. So have lots of respect for what's going on and understand it thoroughly before placing your bets.

BORN Detroit, USA 1926.

EDUCATION Wilson took a MA in Economics from the University of Michigan and spent two years at the University of Michigan Law School.

CAREER Wilson started his career at First Boston Corp. as a trainee, followed by fifteen years at General American Investor (vice-president) and A. G. Becker & Co (voting stockholder). Meanwhile, he managed his own originally modest fund on the side until he was about 40. By then he had made enough money to concentrate exclusively on his own funds. He created a hedge fund for family and friends in the 1970s, but this was never an important part of the funds he managed. He retired in 1986 aged 60.

INVESTMENT PHILOSOPHY Wilson was a speculator or, as he describes himself, long-term trader. He worked with themes, sentiment, concepts rather than realities and fundamental research. He had a very flexible, pragmatic, and humble approach to his strategy. Convinced that short-term techniques worked, but ultimately would fail, he therefore saw the need to change the strategy continuously. Instead of avoiding risk, he sought risk, because that was where you could make money. Preferable investments on the long side were companies that did something new and different, or did it in different way. Technology stocks and smaller stocks in general fit into this description. On the short side he liked equities that were in the middle of a bubble. Unlike momentum traders, he shorted stocks when share prices increased as well as imploded. He almost never visited management and the same went for the analysts, as he regarded them to be too bureaucratic. Most of the day and evening he spent communicating with brokers and other investors, who were the main source of his ideas together with business magazines. One of his golden rules was not to try to anticipate how fast the competition could undercut healthy established companies. It is better to sell a winning stock too late than too soon. His strategy was not suitable for non-professional and conservative investors being too individual and difficult to copy.

OTHER Wilson is one of the hedge-fund titans. He stopped investing after retirement and entrusted his wealth to a dozen money managers. He then started giving money to conservation causes such as the World Monuments Fund, Nature Conservancy, and the Wildlife Conservation Society. Wilson said he has donated more than $600 million to charity and has given away 70 % of his wealth. Despite being an atheist, he has given $30 million to Roman Catholic schools. He loves classical music.

Sources: Robert W. Wilson; John Train, *Money Masters of Our Time* (2000). Forbes; Bloomberg.

NEIL
WOODFORD
UK

ANNUAL YIELD
13%
for **20** YEARS

BENCHMARK 8%

Long term. Taking a long-term view is an increasingly unfashionable approach in today's environment. In recent years, average holding periods for equities have shortened dramatically, reflecting a trading rather than an investing mentality. For me, investing in a company is an ongoing process: it starts with meeting the management team and undertaking in depth research of the business and typically I will build a holding over a period of time. While clearly things can change, my intention is to be a long-term owner of that company; I am not simply seeking a quick return. Many of the companies that are in my portfolios have been there for more than ten years and they continue to deliver the earnings and dividend growth that attracted me to them at the outset. As I alluded to above, markets can be driven by a number of things, and during those periods stocks can be mispriced for a considerable length of time. We saw this in the late 1990s with the TMT bubble and we have also seen it more recently in the post-financial crisis period. However, sooner or later, markets return to valuing companies according to their fundamental characteristics, and so maintaining conviction during

these times and focusing on the long-term is essential to fully participate in the returns that selected companies can provide.

Valuation. My second key element is fundamentals. Simply put, earnings and dividend growth drive share prices in the long term, and so these are the key metrics on which to focus. Dividends are one of the best ways to gauge the health of a business, as well as providing a good insight into the management's capital discipline and recognition of shareholder returns. Research also indicates that those companies with the strongest dividend growth provide the best capital returns in the long term. Therefore, a company's ability to consistently grow its earnings and dividends is a prime consideration in my investment approach. At the same time, a company fulfilling these requirements is not necessarily a good investment. Valuation is critical, and it is where I believe a company's growth potential is not reflected in its valuation that will I consider investing.

Risk. This brings us to the final core element of my investment approach, which is the management of risk. I have an unconstrained approach within the portfolios that

I manage and so I do not view risk as being relative to a benchmark index. To me, risk is the permanent loss of capital, and in that sense I have an absolute return mentality. Risk can never be completely eliminated from equity market investment, but there are steps that can help to reduce it. Understanding risk means understanding the underlying business: what it does, how it earns its profits, and how sustainable are those returns. Gaining this level of insight and knowledge of a company enables me to form an opinion on how that company should be valued. If the conclusion is that the company is undervalued then it represents a lower-risk investment—in other words, valuation is, in itself, an effective risk-management tool.

BORN Berkshire, UK 1960.

EDUCATION Woodford holds a BA in Economics and Agricultural Economics from the University of Exeter; he later studied Finance at the London Business School.

CAREER He commenced his investment career in 1981 with the Dominion Insurance Company, and subsequently joined Eagle Star as a fund manager in 1987. One year later he joined Invesco Perpetual as a fund manager in the UK equities team, and is currently the company's head of investments.

INVESTMENT PHILOSOPHY Woodford is a fundamental long-term bottom-up stock market value investor. He invests mainly in the UK. As follows of his extensive description above, his preference is for resilient companies whose growth and earnings he sees as stable, yet are underappreciated by the market. Not surprisingly he shows the best relative performance in turbulent market conditions. Woodford is something of an activist, pressing managers at companies to pursue share buybacks when the intrinsic value of a company well exceeds its share price.

OTHER As head of investments at Invesco Perpetual, Woodford controls over £25 billion of assets. He has been awarded several prizes. His hobbies include wildlife and horses.

Sources: Neil Woodford; Invesco Perpetual High Income Fund; Wikipedia.

DONALD A.
YACKTMAN
USA

ANNUAL YIELD
10%
for **19** YEARS
BENCHMARK 7%

First, this business basically boils down to what you buy and what you pay for it. Price is critical, so view stocks as bonds and consistently view the investment process as looking for the best risk adjusted forward rates of return. No one can predict the future with absolute certainty, so look at the future cash flows and try to project their growth and how predictable they are, in order to determine those risk-adjusted forward returns and how much the risk premium needs to be so you can be generally right and not wrong to the fourth decimal. By using a process like this, you are slanting the odds in your favour, and should end up most of the time with a portfolio of above-average businesses purchased at below-average prices.

Second, think about the long term and don't worry about the short term. You may not outperform the market every quarter or year but the goal is to outperform it over ten years. Think of investing as a marathon, not a sprint, and have patience. Volatility is the friend of a value investor and creates opportunity. Focus of what you can control and don't spend lots of time on things you can't control.

Third, there is no substitute for knowledge. Make a real effort to understand the business model and what to expect from each business investment under different economic circumstances. Know the strengths and weaknesses of each business investment so you will have the ability to be objective and buy more of it or sell some of it at the appropriate times.

BORN Chicago, USA 1941.

EDUCATION Yacktman holds a B.Sc. magna cum laude in Economics from the University of Utah, and an MBA with distinction from Harvard University.

CAREER He started his investment carrier as portfolio manager at Stein Roe &

Farnham. After fourteen years he moved to Selected Financial Services, where he worked for ten years as a senior portfolio manager. In 1992 he founded Yacktman Asset Management Funds, where he is president and co-chief investment officer.

INVESTMENT PHILOSOPHY He is a bottom-up stock market value investor. Yacktman searches for companies that have high market share, high cash return on tangible assets, a shareholder-friendly management, and selling for a price that is less than what an investor would pay to buy the whole company. The target company should also have growth prospects and sell products or services that have fairly predictable demand in both good times and bad. The strategy usually brings in typically out-of-favour stocks and he uses metaphors such as 'It's easier to pick apples on the ground than in the trees'. Free cashflow yield is an important valuation metric. Yacktman Asset Management operates with a fairly concentrated portfolio with a low turnover where the proportion of liquid assets can at times be high. At companies where he is a stockholder he never meets the management, and he votes down every suggestion to reward the executives with options.

OTHER Yacktman Asset Management has around $12 billion in assets, mainly US large cap. In the last ten years Yacktman's fund has performed yearly 7.5 percentage points better than benchmark. He has won several prizes and was named Portfolio Manager of the Year by Morningstar in 1991. His hobbies are reading biographies and American history.

....

Sources: Donald A. Yacktman; Yacktman Asset Management; Yacktman Fund.

FELIX W. ZULAUF

SWITZERLAND

ANNUAL YIELD

10%

for **22** YEARS

BENCHMARK 2%

Many factors contribute to making you successful in the markets and you first have to find your own way, what works for you, be it company and stock analysis or macro analysis or whatever. The greatest advantage is to have a knowledge of political and economic history. Simply put: try to understand how the system works and then find your analysis or whatever. The best thing is to have an understanding of most aspects and deep knowledge but then finally you must discover what works best for you. Understanding business cycles and having knowledge of how to benefit from it in the markets.

Once you reach this stage, you should develop and have a great passion for markets and a strong curiosity to constantly learn. This keeps you working hard and being focused. Becoming successful in markets is a marathon run through life and not a sprint.

Develop a risk management procedure and technique that helps you to avoid the big mistakes. It should work both ways; taking you out of positions you are long or short on before it hurts very badly but it should also put you into long or short positions to avoid missing big opportunities. At the end of the day, losing a little when wrong and making big money when right is the key to success.

BORN Diessenhofen, Switzerland 1950.

EDUCATION Zulauf graduated from commercial college in Schaffhausen/ Switzerland in 1971.

CAREER Zulauf started as a trader for global markets at Swiss Bank Corporation 1971. After working as both analyst and portfolio manager for several leading investment banks in Paris and New York he joined the Swiss investment bank UBS as mutual fund manager. At UBS he also acted as global investment strategist for the entire group. At age 40 he launched his own company Zulauf Asset Management AG. After almost two decades Zulauf Asset Management was split in two parts where Zulauf fully owns the split-off Zulauf Asset Management focusing on managing primarily his own capital. Moreover, he is Chairman and co-CIO of Vicenda Asset Management AG as consultant to various large investors around the world.

INVESTMENT PHILOSOPHY Zulauf is foremost a low risk top-down macro investor. The foundation in his investment approach comes from his conviction that economies and capital markets are cyclical and not linear and the markets go through long valuation cycles from over- to undervaluation over time spans of 15–25 years. To estimate where in the business cycle the market is and what asset classes should rise or fall he uses a 4-step comprehensive market analysis method: (i) The monetary framework shows what amount of liquidity is available for investments in assets. (ii) Valuation indicates the level of potential risk and reward. (iii) Momentum measures the health of a trend. (iv) Sentiment is best used as a contrary indicator when it goes to extremes.

This view and belief has helped him to preserve capital during difficult times and virtually all bear markets in stocks between 1973 and 2009.

OTHER He has been a member of Barron's Round Table for over 25 years and has together with Marc Faber (p. 86) the far best performance in the recommended portfolio for the last decade among the members. Zulauf is well known in the investment world with multiple accurate investment predictions. Recently he was one of the first to warn about a weaker yen. Outside his profession his interests are in music and sport and he enjoys playing golf to relax.

Sources: Felix W. Zulauf; www.zuam.ch.

MARTIN
ZWEIG
USA

ANNUAL YIELD
16%
for **23** YEARS
BENCHMARK 10%

→ Don't fight the Fed.
→ Don't fight the Tape.
→ Beware of the crowd.

BORN Cleveland, Ohio, USA 1942. Died 2013.

EDUCATION Zweig had a BSE from the Wharton School, an MBA from the University of Miami, and a Ph.D. in Finance from Michigan State University. He later taught finance at Iona College and Baruch College.

CAREER He started his career in the 1970s writing an investment newsletter and articles in Barron's Magazine. He went on to become a successful and influential investment advisor on Wall Street, known for his exhaustive data studies. Zweig later exploited his popularity and success into a thriving asset management business, including several mutual funds. The largest is the hedge fund Associate, which he established in 1985 at the age of 47, and which is still operating today. He quit active trading 2006 but was until recently still chairman of Zweig-DiMenna.

INVESTMENT PHILOSOPHY Zweig is sometimes described as the finance professor who turned into an investment guru by following a simple mantra: 'Don't buck the interest-rate trend'. But it is more sophisticated than that. He was a fundamental, quantitative, and technical investor with a focus on growth. To judge the market as a whole, he gave greater weight to technical analysis than fundamental analysis. He invented and used the well-known put/call ratio that measures the advance/decline ratio and volumes to gauge which direction the market is going to move next. Zweig's basic stock market strategy was to be fully invested in the market when the indications were positive and to sell stocks when indications became negative. Risk minimization and loss limitation were crucial to his strategy. When it comes to judging individual stocks, he gave greater weight to fundamental analysis than technical analysis. He had more than a dozen criteria in selecting stocks. Some of the most important ones were: (i) the company should have annual earnings growth of 20 % or more for at least four years, and sales growth should be similar to earnings growth; (ii) reduce the risk of overpaying for growth by rejecting any companies whose price/earnings ratios are more than 60 % above average for their sector, and also reject companies with a P/E of five or less; (iii) company debt should be average or below average for the sector the company operates in; and (iv) management should not have overestimated the last three years' earnings and there should be no selling of stock by insiders.

Stocks whose fundamentals look attractive were screened using a basic technical analysis. Only stocks whose price action showed strength were selected. Zweig was not a friend of the underdog and he was definitely not one for a buy-and-hold strategy. He did not insist on understanding what a company did or how its products work. Despite all these investment rules, his opinion was that models had to evolve – no indicator works forever. His famous quote from the book Winning on Wall Street, says as much: 'People somehow think you must buy at the bottom and sell at the top to be successful in the market. That's nonsense. The idea is to buy when the probability is greatest that the market is going to advance'.

OTHER Like Peter Lynch, Zweig was another 'legendary' investor who decided to step out of the limelight while he was at the top of his game. Several independent institutions and investors simulating famous investors' strategies claim that Zweig's strategy shows the best performance of all investors both past and present. The inspiration for a number of his methods, according to Zweig himself came from Jesse Livermore. Zweig started buying stocks as a teenager. In 1986, he published the best-selling Winning on Wall Street. Zweig was widely known as the Wall Street tycoon who had the most expensive single-family residence in the country – an apartment in Manhattan bought for $70 million. He also owned Buddy Holly's guitar.

Sources: Martin Zweig, *Winning on Wall Street* (1986); Zweig-DiMenna; The American Association of Individual Investors; Wikipedia.

HÜSNÜ ÖZYEĞIN
TURKEY

THE MOST SUCCESSFUL INVESTOR IN TURKEY

→ Invest in businesses either you or your trusted team members know and understand.

→ Be patient with your investments. If you believe you have made the right investment stick to your bet.

→ Do not get emotional about your investments and try to hang on to them for extended periods. When the market becomes irrational, sell your investment and wait for another opportunity.

BORN Ismir, Turkey 1944.

EDUCATION Özyeğin holds a B.Sc. in Civil Engineering from Oregon State University and an MBA from Harvard Business School.

CAREER After a brief stint with IBM and Arthur D. Little in the US, Özyeğin returned to Turkey in 1974. He became general manager of Pamukbank in 1977 and eight years later of Yapı ve Kredi Bankası, which he led until 1987, when he decided to establish his own bank, Finansbank, at the age of 43. He later brought all finance assets under the name of Fiba Holding, where he serves as chairman.

INVESTMENT PHILOSOPHY Özyeğin is both an entrepreneur and a long-term pragmatic investor. His deals are mainly done outside the stock market and he usually buys entire companies. What is perhaps the most impressive thing about his investment skill is his timing. In 2006, Özyeğin sold Finansbank to the National Bank of Greece at a price of $5.5 billion, of which he received $3.2 billion. What would the price have been today? He stayed away from the banking sector until 2010. Even if the finance sector is his home turf, he has been successful in other areas as well, such as retail, real estate, and energy. All these timely acquisitions and exits demonstrate a profound knowledge of society and macroeconomics, as well as courage and stamina.

OTHER At the moment Özyeğin owns almost eighty companies round the globe. He claims that he went to the US with just a thousand dollars in his pocket. At present Forbes estimates his wealth to be $3 billion – a compounded rate of return of 38 % annually for forty-six years. This self-made billionaire's performance even tops the performance of Warren Buffett. Özyeğin has spent $100 million building thirty-six primary schools and girls' dormitories in the poorest parts of Turkey. He plans to spend up to $1 billion over the next fifteen years on the Özyeğin University in Istanbul and other philanthropic activities.

Sources: Hüsnü Özyeğin; FIBA Holding; Wikipedia.

NASSER MOHAMMED
AL-KHARAFI
KUWAIT

Nasser Mohammed Al-Kharafi (1943–2012) passed away during the work with this book, before he had shared his investment strategy with me. However he managed to send me his insights, as follow.

Take good care of the people around you. I have always believed in people and their needs, whether they are fellow-workers or clients. You can't demand results or loyalty unless all parts of the puzzle fit together. Taking care of the people working with me or with whom I have to deal is high on my list of priorities in my work. By offering them all conceivable comfort and security I get them to have trust in me and enable them to to be creative and do their best.

Integrity in your dealings is important. It is always a privilege and of great value to be honest, open and straightforward in all your dealings. A dishonest person can never succeed in the long run. Dishonesty will bring you down in the end.

Calculate the risks you take. Business is based on entrepreneurship and risk-taking. Without any sort of risk you will never succeed or have a cutting edge. A person who never takes risks is a person with no experience. But the risks have to be calculated and measured and the narrow line between calculated risk and immature risk has to be carefully identified and respected.

Sources: Nasser Mohammed Al-Kharafi.

THANKS

This book would have been impossible without the help of a great many people across the world. In everything from finding prospective interviewees to verifying yields, I have not worked alone. Three people in particular have gone above and beyond the call of duty. Ragnar Kämpe, Christer Jakobson, and Göran Ivemark have been tireless in their encouragement and generous with their wise comments and close reading of the manuscript. Without Ragnar's advice and energy, I doubt the book would have seen the light of day. Christer's razor-sharp analytical skills saved me from any number of intellectual pitfalls. Göran's enthusiastic discussions brought a whole new dimension to my work. Thank you for all your efforts.

I also wish to thank my publishers, Roos & Tegnér, who have seen my work into print: without my editor Erika Feldt, I would have been lost. I also owe a debt of thanks to my nearest and dearest, and especially my Louise, who has supported me through all the ups and downs of the project.

And above all I wish to thank all the investors who generously took the time to share their experiences, insights, and strategies. This despite the fact that it is statistically proven that successful investment models work less well once they become widely known. That some of them prioritized their contributions to the book despite failing health is further reason for my heartfelt gratitude.

Magnus Angenfelt, Lidingö, January 2013